Listen LOVE REPEAT

OTHER-CENTERED LIVING
IN A SELF-CENTERED WORLD

STUDY GUIDE | SIX SESSIONS

KAREN EHMAN

ZONDERVAN®

ZONDERVAN

Listen, Love, Repeat Study Guide
Copyright © 2016 by Karen Ehman

This title is also available as a Zondervan ebook.

ISBN 978-0-310-08264-4

Requests for information should be addressed to:
Zondervan, *3900 Sparks Dr. SE, Grand Rapids, Michigan 49546*

Published in association with the literary agency of The FEDD Agency, Inc., Post Office Box 341973, Austin, TX 78734.

Art direction: Brian Bobel
Interior design: Denise Froehlich

First Printing September 2016 / Printed in the United States of America

Contents

How to Use This Guide
5

SESSION 1:
Finding Your Big "Why?"
9

SESSION 2:
Let Love Complete the Circle
31

SESSION 3:
When You Live a Life of Welcome
53

SESSION 4:
How to Hug a Porcupine and Squeeze a Skunk
73

SESSION 5:
Family Matters
93

SESSION 6:
The Boomerang of Blessing
113

Bonus Session Leader Instructions
135

BONUS SESSION 7:
Other-Centered Living in a Self-Centered World
139

Quips and Quotables
152

Gift Tags
155

Session Challenges
156

Scripture Memory Verses
157

How to Use This Guide

Group Size

The *Listen, Love, Repeat* video curriculum is designed to be experienced in a group setting such as a Bible study, Sunday school class, or any small group gathering. After viewing each video together, members will participate in a group discussion. Ideally, discussion groups should be no larger than twelve people. You will notice occasional portions of the discussion where you are encouraged to break into smaller clusters of three to six people each for more heart-to-heart sharing and Scripture study. These times are clearly noted in the guide.

Materials Needed

Each participant should have her own study guide, which includes video outline notes, directions for activities, and discussion questions, as well as a reading plan and personal studies to deepen learning between sessions. Participants are also strongly encouraged to have a copy of the *Listen, Love, Repeat* book. Reading the book alongside the video curriculum provides even deeper insights that make the journey richer and more meaningful (also, a few of the questions pertain to material covered in the book). Noted that there are also additional materials needed for a bonus session wrap-up party (see pages 135–140).

Timing

The time notations–for example (23 minutes)–indicate the *actual* time of video segments and the *suggested* time for each activity or discussion. Adhering to the suggested times will enable you to complete each session in an hour and fifteen minutes. If you have additional time, bonus questions are provided, thereby expanding the session to an hour and a half, or even longer if your group desires. If you are serving refreshments and including prayer time, figure another thirty minutes.

Facilitation

Each group should appoint a facilitator who is responsible for starting the video and for keeping track of time during discussions and activities. Facilitators may also read questions aloud and monitor discussions, prompting members to respond and ensuring that everyone has the opportunity to participate.

Between-Sessions Personal Study

Maximize the impact of the course with additional study between group sessions. Carving out about two hours total for personal study between meeting times will enable you to complete both the book and between-session studies by the end of the course. For each session, you may wish to complete the personal study all in one sitting or to spread it out over a few days (for example, working on it a half hour a day on four different days that week). PLEASE NOTE: If you are unable to finish (or even start!) your between-sessions personal study, still attend the group study video session. We are all busy and life happens. You are still wanted and welcome at class even if you don't have your "homework" done.

Session Challenges

Every session offers a simple challenge for listening and loving, which can be summed up in a short, easy-to-remember phrase. In order for the challenge to be prominent in your mind throughout the week, we have printed each one on page 156 for you to photocopy, cut out, and place where you will see it frequently. Or you can type the phrase, making it the screen saver on your computer or the lock screen on your phone.

Scripture Memory

Each study also includes a key Scripture verse that highlights the session theme. If you wish to maximize your learning experience, consider memorizing these verses. In order to assist you with this goal, all six verses are printed on pages 157–158 of the study guide.

Photocopy this page on paper or card stock and then cut out the appropriate verses week by week. (You really creative and crafty types may even want to use scrapbooking paper to layer them on top of some decorative paper.) Then keep them in a handy place—perhaps your car, pocketbook, or laptop bag. You can practice memorizing them while waiting in the car-pool line or at the doctor's office. Or post them at your kitchen sink or on your bathroom mirror where you will see them each day. Laminating them will help to keep them from getting ruined if they get splashed.

It may be helpful to have the group facilitator inquire if any participants are attempting to memorize the key verses. Perhaps those members will want to show up five minutes early (or stay after for a few minutes) to practice reciting them to each other.

Finding Your Big "Why?"

"In the same way, let your light shine before others, that they may see your good deeds and glorify your Father in heaven."

(MATTHEW 5:16)

——— Video: Finding Your Big "Why?" (23 minutes) ———

Play the video teaching segment for session one. As you watch, record any thoughts or concepts that stand out to you in the outline that follows.

NOTES

One of the oldest questions known to humans might very well be, "Why am I here?"

_____

_____

_____

_____

Summum bonum is a Latin expression meaning "the highest good"–an end in itself that also encompasses all other goods in life.

_____

_____

_____

_____

Karen's mentor believes that we are on Earth for two reasons: to have a relationship with God, who offers us a place in heaven, and to take every opportunity to point others to Jesus so they will spend eternity in heaven too.

_____

_____

_____

_____

Although Jesus was the Son of God and on a very big mission, Jesus was never too busy to notice. He lived alert.

_____

_____

_____

_____

Jesus wasn't about doing *big things*. He was about doing the *right thing*. And often for him, the right thing was noticing one simple soul. Mark 5:21–34 tells the story of the synagogue ruler Jairus and the woman with the bleeding disorder. We learn from this story the following:

♥ Jesus didn't draw attention to himself. Scripture simply says, "So Jesus went with him."

♥ The simple, frantic touch of the woman did not escape Jesus' notice.

♥ The woman in this story wasn't important, as Jairus was. We aren't told her title or even her name.

♥ Jesus is calling us to live alert. For Jesus, ministry usually was the person he found standing right in front of him.

_____

_____

_____

_____

We need to make relationships our big "Why?" We need to learn to value people over possessions. And value people over positions.

_____

_____

_____

_____

"When you are in the final days of your life, what will you want? Will you hug that college degree in the walnut frame? Will you ask to be carried to the garage so you can sit in your car? Will you find comfort in rereading your financial statement? Of course not. What will matter then will be people. If relationships will matter most then, shouldn't they matter most now?"–Max Lucado

_____

_____

_____

_____

How do we behave if relationships are our "Why?" for being alive?

_____

_____

_____

_____

We need to learn to hear a heart drop: to listen between the lines when someone is speaking, to really hear their heart.

_____

_____

_____

_____

When loving others, we must keep in mind Matthew 5:14–16: "You are the light of the world. A town built on a hill cannot be hidden. Neither do people light a lamp and put it under a bowl. Instead they put it on its stand, and it gives light to everyone in the house. In the same way, let your light shine before others, that they may see your good deeds and glorify your Father in heaven."

_____

_____

_____

_____

We don't do good works in order to be noticed. We don't do them to say, "Look at me!" We do them in order to say, "Well, will you look at him!"

_____

_____

_____

_____

Here is an upside-down truth: if you want to find your life, first you need to lose it. Matthew 16:25 urges, "For whoever wants to save their life will lose it, but whoever loses their life for me will find it."

_____

_____

_____

_____

Piglet sidled up to Pooh from behind. "Pooh!" he whispered. "Yes, Piglet?" "Nothing," said Piglet, taking Pooh's paw. "I just wanted to be sure of you."

A. A. Milne, *The House at Pooh Corner* G

Group Discussion (8 minutes)

Take a few minutes to discuss what you just watched.

1. What part of the video teaching had the most impact on you?

_____

_____

_____

_____

2. Have you ever heard of the philosophical concept of *summum bonum? It is a* Latin expression meaning "the highest good"–an end in itself that also encompasses all other goods in life. What do you think of the idea of deciding your own *summum bonum* in life?

_____

_____

_____

_____

3. Discuss your thoughts on the two reasons why Karen's mentor thinks we are on earth: to have a relationship with God, who offers us a place in heaven, and to take every opportunity to point others to Jesus so they will spend eternity in heaven too.

_____

_____

_____

_____

─────── **Cluster Group Discussion (8 minutes)** ───────

If your group is comprised of more than twelve members, consider completing this discussion in smaller groups of three to six people each.

4. Grab your Bibles and turn to Mark chapter 5. Have someone read verses 21–34 aloud to the group. In the space below, record as many observations as you can about the following:

♥ List all the people (or groups of people) who were physically present in the story, even if they never spoke a word but only observed.

_____

_____

_____

_____

♥ Next, list any adjectives (excited, angry, etc.) that describe how each of the people (or group of people) must have felt watching this scene unfold.

_____

_____

_____

_____

♥ Are there any guidelines you can draw out of this passage for living alert? Who was Jesus most concerned with when this scene took place—the crowds or the unnamed ill woman? What does this teach us about how we should behave today?

_____

_____

_____

_____

——————— **Group Discussion (15 minutes)** ———————

Gather back together as one large group and answer the following questions.

5. What is one insight you gained from the small group activity on Mark 5?

    _____

    _____

    _____

    _____

6. What people in the Mark 5 passage were mentioned but not physically present? (See verses 23 and 26.) How might the news of this story have affected them when they heard it?

    _____

    _____

    _____

    _____

7. In the video segment, Karen talked about the concept that for Jesus, often his greatest ministry was the person he found standing in front of him. Who are some people you often find standing in front of you on any given day? Do you tend to see them as someone to minister to or someone who is an interruption or even a nuisance? Be honest.

    _____

    _____

    _____

    _____

8. Karen talked about how often we tend to value possessions over people or place position over people. Why do you think we do this—placing a higher value on our stuff or our status than on our relationships?

    _____

    _____

    _____

9. In the video, we were introduced to the concept of hearing a "heart drop"—listening between the lines. Can you think of a time when someone you know heard you give a "heart drop" and did something special to cheer you up or encourage you? Share it with the group.

_____

_____

_____

_____

10. BONUS QUESTION: Only when we love and share and serve, as Scripture commands us, can we live life on purpose, embracing the big "Why?"—the reason God brought us to Earth in the first place. Discuss the concept of upside-down living. This type of living says, "If you want to feel significant, you need to embrace obscurity and instead make others feel significant." How have you found this to be true?

_____

_____

_____

_____

11. BONUS QUESTION: Have someone read Matthew 5:14–16 aloud. Do you know of a situation in which someone's good deeds glorified God in such a way that another person was led to have a relationship with Christ? Share with the group what happened.

_____

_____

_____

_____

12. BONUS QUESTION: What did you think of the story of "J"—the elderly man who interrupted Karen's writing of this very Bible study? Has there ever been someone in your life like this, maybe a lonely neighbor or a needy coworker?

Share honestly with the group what happened and how you felt when that person seemed to take up a lot of your time.

_____

_____

_____

_____

Knowing what you have learned today during this study, how might you react differently if the same scenario happened today? What can you say to yourself in the future when you are trying to get work done—or even just trying to relax—and another soul seems lonely or in need of some help or encouragement?

_____

_____

_____

_____

— Individual Activity: What Is God Asking Me to Do? (5 minutes) —

Complete this activity on your own.

Take a moment to think through your current relationships—both inside and outside your home. The relationships may be with an individual or with a group—such as your students (if you are a teacher) or the neighborhood kids. List these people, and groups of people, in the spaces below.

_____   _____

_____   _____

_____   _____

_____   _____

Now, go back and put a star before the one or two people or groups you most tend to view as an interruption or even a nuisance rather than someone to whom you can minister. Ask God to help you change your perspective in the future.

──────── **Session 1 Memory Verse (1 minute)** ────────

Each session has a corresponding—and completely optional—Scripture memory verse or passage. Members may be interested in coming to the study five minutes early to practice reciting their verses with others; if so, coordinate that now.

Then, as a group, read aloud this session's memory verse:

> "In the same way, let your light shine before others, that they may see your good deeds and glorify your Father in heaven."
>
> (MATTHEW 5:16)

──────── **Challenge Reminder and Closing Prayer (2 minutes)** ────────

CHALLENGE: LIVE ALERT! Remember this week to live alert. In your between-sessions study, write this on a sticky note, make it your computer's screen saver or cell phone lock screen, or photocopy the ready-made reminder found on page 156. Then, make it your aim to live alert this week, listening for heart drops.

PRAYER: Have one person close in prayer, focusing on learning to live alert, hear those heart drops, and view people not as interruptions but as opportunities for ministry as Jesus did. Then, get ready to learn more in your between-sessions personal study prior to session two!

Between-Sessions Personal Study

SESSION 1

LIVE ALERT! Remember this week to live alert. Take a moment right now to write that phrase on a sticky note and post it where you will see it often or make those two words the screen saver on your computer or lock screen of your phone. Or, for your convenience, simply photocopy the ready-made challenge phrase found on page 156. Then, make it your aim to live alert this week, listening for heart drops.

Session 1 Memory Verse

Below is the memory verse for this session. (For your convenience, designed versions of all verses are printed in the back of this study guide beginning on page 157.) You may photocopy those pages on card stock or colored paper. Then, cut out the verses and place them in a prominent place—purse, dashboard, desk, kitchen sink—where you can read, study, or memorize. (You may want to laminate them if posting them at your kitchen or bathroom sink.) Place each verse where you have easy access to it throughout the day. Set an alarm for at least two times a day when you know you will have a minute to look over the verse and commit it to memory.

> "In the same way, let your light shine before others, that they may see your good deeds and glorify your Father in heaven."
>
> (MATTHEW 5:16)

Read and Learn

Read chapters 1–2 of the *Listen, Love, Repeat* book. Use the space below to record any insights you discovered or questions you may want to bring to the next group session.

_____

_____

_____

_____

_____

_____

_____

Study and Reflect

1. Have you ever known someone who you would say lived alert—constantly on the lookout for anyone who might need encouragement? Jot down a few sentences about this person and what impact their actions had on others, including you.

_____

_____

_____

_____

2. In chapter one of *Listen, Love, Repeat*, Karen writes this about the story of Jesus, Jairus, and the unnamed ill woman in Mark 5:

> Could we try to be more like Jesus, this perfect man who was never too busy to notice someone who needed his touch? Sure, we also have many things calling for our attention. Crowds of people and projects press in. Whether at work or at home, we are often on our way to do something grand. But Jesus is calling us to stop and notice. To live alert. To give a special touch that may heal a heart or cheer a weary soul.
>
> I once heard it said that Jesus' real ministry was the person he found standing in front of him. Who is that for *you* today?
>
> LISTEN, LOVE, REPEAT, PAGE 19

♥ Have you ever been in the middle of something big when someone seemingly insignificant needed to be noticed? If so, describe the situation here:

_____

_____

_____

♥ How does this concept of ministry being the person standing in front of you inspire, challenge—or even frustrate—you?

_____

_____

_____

_____

♥ Think back on Jesus' interaction with the synagogue ruler Jairus in Mark 5. Focus in on verse 24. What does the first phrase in that verse say? Write it out here.

_____

_____

_____

♥ Next, write the following on a sticky note or piece of scrap paper and post it where you will see it often this week: "Who in my life needs me to stop what I am doing and 'go with them'?"

♥ Finally, using a scale of 1 to 10 (with 1 being "never" and 10 being "always"), use the chart on the next page to evaluate each area of your life when it comes to being intentional to listen to the spoken—and unspoken—needs of those people. They may be family members, coworkers, friends, or an acquaintance you know from a church or community activity. Record your rating in column two. Jot a phrase or two about what might be a physical or emotional need of theirs in column three. (You may need additional space if you have more family or work relationships than allowed for on the chart.)

Area	Rating:	What they might need physically or emotionally:
Spouse:		
Child:		
Child:		
Child:		
Child:		
Child:		
Extended family member:		
Extended family member:		
Extended family member:		
Extended family member:		
Coworker:		
Coworker:		
Coworker:		
Friend:		
Friend:		
Friend:		
Friend:		
Neighbor:		
Neighbor:		
Acquaintance:		
Acquaintance:		
Other:		
Other:		
Other:		
Other:		

♥ What did you learn from the preceding exercise? Are there certain people with whom it is easier for you to be attentive than others? Why do you think that is?

_____

_____

_____

_____

♥ What people or projects call for your attention today, pressing in close? What is one thing you can remind yourself of in the future when you are feeling crowded but find someone in need of some encouragement standing in your midst?

_____

_____

_____

_____

> People all around us every day are longing for someone to notice them. They may feel alone or ashamed. Afraid or apprehensive. The simple act of noticing someone as he or she journeys through life can lovingly mirror the behavior of God. But in order to behave like Jesus did, and spread the healing balm of his love, we must be willing to drop our agenda—or at least put it on hold—to reach out and touch those who need it most.
>
> LISTEN, LOVE, REPEAT, PAGE 20

3. In chapter one of *Listen, Love, Repeat* (page 22) we read this passage of Scripture:

> Through Jesus, therefore, let us continually offer to God a sacrifice of praise—the fruit of lips that openly profess his name. And do not forget to do good and to share with others, for with such sacrifices God is pleased.
>
> (HEBREWS 13:15–16)

Karen then writes:

> *I see in this verse three simple ways to spread love:*
> 1. *Praise God by professing his name with our lips.*
> 2. *Do good.*
> 3. *Share with others.*
>
> *And what is the result of our performing these straightforward actions? Pleasing God.*

Which of the above three steps comes most naturally for you? Which is the hardest? In which one would you most like to see improvement? Write your answers below.

_____

_____

_____

4. Matthew 22:37 reads, "Love the Lord your God with all your heart and with all your soul and with all your mind." In chapter two of *Listen, Love, Repeat* (page 39), Karen writes:

> *If we truly love God with our hearts and souls and minds, we will want to get to know him through the pages of Scripture. We will long to spend time with him in prayer. We will hunger to get to know his heart and mind as we seek to discover his will for our lives. And as we interact with God through prayer and experience his heart through studying the Scriptures, we will learn how to live properly.*

Several spiritual practices associated with loving God are listed in the chart that follows. In the first column, look at the practice and think about your current consistency in this area. Then, in the second column, write a few words or phrases that describe your thoughts. One has already been done as an example for you:

Area of My Walk with God	Description
EXAMPLE: *Bible reading and study*	EXAMPLE: *Read Bible 2–3 times a week; in a weekly Bible study*
Bible reading and study	
Bible memorization	
Prayer–private and corporate	
Worship–private and corporate	
Serving others	
Giving money to God's work	
Fasting (from food or something else I love in order to spend time focusing on God)	

IMPORTANT: We must realize that God's love is not dependent upon our performance or how many things we "do" for him. However, we do show our love for the Lord by obeying his commands. Jesus said in John 14:23, "Anyone who loves me will obey my teaching." Look back over the chart and circle the spiritual practice (or two) in which you feel you most need to be more consistent. Next, in the space provided below write a "goal in a sentence" for the area or areas you circled. Be specific. For example, "I want to begin to get up fifteen minutes earlier each day to spend time memorizing verses or passages from the Bible." Or, "I will begin to keep a prayer journal and spend fifteen minutes each evening recording prayer requests, praying, and also recording the outcomes of those prayers."

_____

_____

_____

_____

> One of the oldest questions known to humans might very well be, "Why am I here?" Something deep within us longs to know the meaning of life. Is there a point to it? And if so, what is it? Where do I fit in the grand scheme of things? And if I am on Earth for a purpose, how do I find it? We simply do not want to go through life having missed our cause and calling.
>
> LISTEN, LOVE, REPEAT, PAGE 35

5. In chapter two of *Listen, Love, Repeat* (pages 50–54), Karen discusses the numerous "one another" commands in Scripture that tell us how we are—or are not—to treat each other. The proper treatment of each other is a visible way to reflect God's love to the watching world. Look up John 13:34–35 and then rewrite it here using your own words:

_____

_____

_____

_____

6. Look up the following Bible passages that also use the phrase "one another." After each, write the word or two that first popped into your mind when you read the verse. It may be an adjective that describes the difficulty or ease of carrying out that command. Maybe it will be the name of a person. Simply write down the first few words that come to mind about each verse.

♥ 1 Thessalonians 5:11

_____

_____

♥ Romans 12:10

_____

_____

♥ 1 Peter 3:8

_____

_____

♥ James 5:9

_____

_____

♥ 1 Corinthians 1:10

_____

_____

♥ Hebrews 13:1

_____

_____

♥ Ephesians 4:32

_____

_____

♥ Romans 12:16

_____

_____

♥ X marks the spot! Based on the "one another" verses you just read in Scripture, how are you doing in the proper treatment of your fellow humans? Place an X on the continuum below that best describes your behavior toward others:

I rarely have an issue treating others properly.	I do an average job treating others as the "one another" commands instruct.	I have a long way to go when it comes to obeying "one another" commands.

♥ Now, are there any adjustments you need to make to your behavior in order to align it more closely with the above verses? If so, what are they?

_____

_____

_____

_____

Scripture Memory Verse of the Week Reminder

Don't forget to work on your memory verse for this week (see page 20). Consider pairing with another study group member to help you stay accountable to memorize all six verses in the *Listen, Love, Repeat* study. You could come a few minutes early to each meeting—or stay a bit longer—to practice your verses with each other.

Let Love Complete the Circle

"A new command I give you: Love one another. As I have loved you, so you must love one another. By this everyone will know that you are my disciples, if you love one another."

(JOHN 13:34–35)

———————— Checking In (10 minutes) ————————

Welcome to session two of *Listen, Love, Repeat*. An important part of this study is sharing what you have learned from reading the book and from completing your between-sessions personal study. Remember, don't worry if you weren't able to cover all the material. It doesn't matter if you are doing the memory verses or not. You are still welcome at the study, and your input is valuable!

♥ What from the session one video segment most challenged or encouraged you since the group last met together?

_____

_____

_____

_____

♥ What insights did you discover by reading chapters 1–2 of the *Listen, Love, Repeat* book? Anything you highlighted or just couldn't get out of your mind?

_____

_____

_____

_____

♥ What stood out to you from the questions and activities in the between-sessions personal study?

_____

_____

_____

_____

♥ Did last session's "Challenge of the Week" (putting the phrase "Live Alert" on a sticky note, screen saver, lock screen, or using the ready-made one from the back of this guide) help you to be more attentive to others? Did you hear a "heart drop"? Share with the group your experience on this challenge to live alert.

_____

_____

_____

_____

_____

──────── Video: Let Love Complete the Circle (23 minutes) ────────

Play the video teaching segment for session two. As you watch, record any thoughts or concepts that stand out to you in the outline that follows.

NOTES

Necessary people are those people in our lives who help us to get life done. Have you ever stopped for a moment to verbally thank one of them on a random, ordinary day?

_____

_____

_____

_____

When we show love to the necessary people in our lives we are acknowledging the fact that all the humans we see are created in the image of God (Genesis 1:26–27).

_____

_____

_____

_____

The golden rule (Matthew 7:12) says, "Do to others what you would have them do to you." Think about our necessary people and what they would love to have done to them.

_____

_____

_____

_____

_____

John 13:34–35 says, "A new command I give you: Love one another. As I have loved you, so you must love one another. By this everyone will know that you are my disciples, if you love one another." This passage does *not* say any of the following:

♥ **By this everyone will know that you are my disciples** . . . if you post lots of Bible verses and inspirational Christian quotes on social media—of course with a lovely picture of a beach or the mountains—or with your Bible, snuggled up next to a mug of coffee.

♥ **By this everyone will know that you are my disciples** . . . if you try to break the record for attending the most Bible studies, watching the most sermons online, downloading the most Christian podcasts, or reading all the latest Christian books.

♥ **By this everyone will know that you are my disciples** . . . if you picket and protest against certain sins—whether in person or just on Facebook.

♥ **By this everyone will know that you are my disciples** . . . if you intentionally and diligently only hang around other Christians.

_____

_____

_____

_____

_____

British Missionary C. T. Studd declared, "Some wish to stay within the sound of church or chapel bell. I'd rather run a rescue shop within a yard of hell."

_____

_____

_____

_____

A very popular verse, John 3:16, shows God's immense love for us. However, another portion of Scripture which is not so popular is 1 John 3:16—it shows how we respond to God's love for us by loving and helping others.

_____

_____

_____

_____

First John 4:7–12 is a portion of Scripture that actually combines the thoughts of both John 3:16 and 1 John 3:16.

_____

_____

_____

_____

Loving others completes the circle—the circle of God demonstrating his love by sending Jesus to die as a sacrifice for our sins and then us sacrificing our time and our money to love other people as an act of worship back up to God. First John 4:12 says, "If we love one another, God lives in us and his love is made complete in us." Can you carve out time this week to love others, performing a simple act in a sacred way?

_____

_____

_____

―――――――― Group Discussion (10 minutes) ――――――――

Take a few minutes to discuss what you just watched.

1. What part of the video teaching had the most impact on you?

_____

_____

_____

_____

2. Take turns rattling off one at a time—popcorn style—various "necessary people" in your life. Has anyone in the group ever done something for a necessary person to show them love—not on a holiday or special occasion—but on a random, ordinary day? If so, what was it?

_____

_____

_____

_____

   Next, have the facilitator of the group throw out the title of a necessary person. Brainstorm as a group various things you could do or words you could say to that person to encourage them and reflect God's love. Do this exercise for five or six different necessary people.

_____

_____

_____

_____

3. Have someone read aloud John 13:34–35. Then discuss the following:

   Jesus said, "By this everyone will know that you are my disciples, if you love one another" (verse 35). What are your thoughts about the ways our current Christian culture seems to have abandoned the second half of this verse, swapping it out for one or more of the statements below? Discuss each concept one at a time. Have you ever witnessed Christians behaving this way? Have you yourself lived in such a way as to make any of these ideas more important than loving others?

♥ **By this everyone will know that you are my disciples** . . . if you post lots of Bible verses and inspirational Christian quotes on social media–of course with a lovely picture of a beach or the mountains–or with your Bible, snuggled up next to a mug of coffee.

♥ **By this everyone will know that you are my disciples** . . . if you try to break the record for attending the most Bible studies, watching the most sermons online, downloading and listening to the most popular Christian podcasts, or reading all the latest Christian books.

♥ **By this everyone will know that you are my disciples** . . . if you picket and protest against certain sins–whether in person or just on Facebook.

♥ **By this everyone will know that you are my disciples** . . . if you intentionally and diligently only hang around other Christians.

_____

_____

_____

_____

——————— Cluster Group Discussion (5 minutes) ———————

If your group is comprised of more than twelve members, consider completing this discussion in smaller groups of three to six people each.

4. Have someone read aloud the following passages . . . slowly so you can really listen to the thoughts conveyed.

♥ John 3:16

♥ 1 John 3:16–18

♥ 1 John 4:7–12

In the video, Karen said that loving others "completes the circle." Using the three passages you just read, as a group write out a few sentences that describe the circle that includes God loving us, us loving God, and then us loving others.

_____

_____

_____

_____

———————————— Group Discussion (15 minutes) ————————————

Gather back together as one large group and answer the following questions.

5. Take turns reading aloud the various answers the smaller cluster groups wrote to question 4. How does the image of a completed circle of love help you understand your purpose here on Earth as it relates to the three types of love found in these verses–God loving us, us loving God, and us loving one another? Have you ever thought about this as a circle before?

_____

_____

_____

_____

6. We are called to love others. The Bible says much about loving and serving our fellow Christians, but we are also called to rub shoulders with those who do not claim to know Christ. Have someone read the following verses aloud. Then, as a group, discuss guidelines we might adopt for close relationships with other believers as well as our interactions with those who do not follow Christ.

♥ Ecclesiastes 4:9–10

_____

_____

♥ Hebrews 10:24–25

_____

_____

♥ Proverbs 27:17

_____

_____

♥ Colossians 4:5–6

_____

_____

♥ 1 Peter 3:15

_____

_____

♥ 1 Corinthians 15:33

_____

_____

♥ Proverbs 12:26

_____

_____

♥ Psalm 1:1–2

_____

_____

♥ Proverbs 22:24–25

_____

_____

♥ 2 Corinthians 6:14

_____

_____

7. Karen told the story of her regret over being too busy to reach out to her nine-doors-down neighbor who committed suicide. Can you think of a time in your life when you regretted being too busy to reach out and get to know someone

or to stop and do something to encourage that person. If you have such a story, briefly tell it.

_____

_____

_____

_____

8. BONUS QUESTION: Instead of waiting to hear of a death, illness, or tragedy, be proactive. Think about your life. Who do you see each week? Each day? Maybe just once a month or so? Is there anyone you feel God might be nudging you to reach out to? Who and why? Share your answer with the group.

_____

_____

_____

_____

9. BONUS QUESTION: British missionary C. T. Studd declared, "Some wish to stay within the sound of church or chapel bell. I'd rather run a rescue shop within a yard of hell." Have you ever known a Christian whose lifestyle seems patterned after C. T. Studd—someone who very intentionally spends time with those who do not know Christ? Tell about this person.

_____

_____

_____

_____

How about you? Do you make it a point to spend time getting to know people who do not claim to be believers? If so, who and why? If not, why do you think you haven't made this a priority?

_____

_____

_____

_____

We can purpose to go deeper—beyond a hurried "Hi!" to an authentic "How are you?"

When God knocks on our hearts, we can knock on their doors.

Will you do it? Will you try? Then once you've reached out, leave the results to God. Our job is obedience. God will do the rest.

Trust me, it is awful to get to know your neighbor through the tales and tears of her relatives at a memorial service.

May we all respond to those taps on our hearts today and not ignore them. God just may use us as he saves a life.

After all, remember it isn't that far of a walk. . . . It's just nine doors down.

LISTEN, LOVE, REPEAT, PAGES 75–76

— Individual Activity: What Is God Asking Me to Do? (3 minutes) —

Complete this activity on your own.

Think of a necessary person in your life who might be in need of some love and encouragement. Spend a moment praying for them and then write down one or two ideas for how you might reach out to this person and show them God's love.

My necessary person: _____

My ideas for outreach:

_____

_____

_____

_____

_____

―――――― **Session 2 Memory Verse (1 minute)** ――――――

As a group, read aloud this session's memory verse:

> A new command I give you: Love one another. As I
> have loved you, so you must love one another. By this
> everyone will know that you are my disciples, if you
> love one another.

(JOHN 13:34–35)

―――― **Challenge Reminder and Closing Prayer (3 minutes)** ――――

CHALLENGE: This week's challenge is to "Make their day." Think of one necessary person in your life who helps you or someone in your family to get life done. Then, do something kind for that person to show your appreciation.

PRAYER: Have one person close the group in prayer, focusing on loving the necessary people in your lives. Then, get ready to learn more in your between-sessions personal study prior to session three!

Between-Sessions Personal Study

SESSION 2

Challenge Reminder

This week's challenge is to "Make their day." Think of one necessary person in your life who helps you or someone in your family to get life done. Then, think of something kind to do to show your appreciation. Record who the person is and what you plan to do for them in your calendar—whether the one on your phone or your paper one.

Session 2 Memory Verse

Below is the memory verse for this session. Write it on a note card, type it in the notes app on your phone, or photocopy the ready-made one found in the back of this guide on page 157. Set an alarm for at least two times a day when you know you will have a minute to look over the verse and commit it to memory.

> A new command I give you: Love one another. As I have loved you, so you must love one another. By this everyone will know that you are my disciples, if you love one another.

(JOHN 13:34–35)

Read and Learn

Read chapters 3–4 of the *Listen, Love, Repeat* book. Use the space below to record any insights you discovered or questions you may want to bring to the next group session.

_____

_____

_____

_____

_____

_____

Study and Reflect

1. In chapter three of *Listen, Love, Repeat*, Karen told of her friend Mary driving from a state away to attend Karen's father-in-law's funeral, and how much that

meant to her. Can you think of an instance when someone in your life did something that cost him or her a lot of time and really touched your heart? Briefly describe it here.

_____

_____

_____

_____

2. On pages 64–65 of the book *Listen, Love, Repeat,* Karen writes about the apostle Paul and his relationship with the Christians in Thessalonica. The book of 1 Thessalonians was written by Paul and opened with a greeting from not only him but also from his co-laborers in the church, Silas and Timothy. Read 1 Thessalonians 2:7–8 and answer the questions below based on this passage.

♥ What does the image of a nursing mother caring for her children portray when it comes to Paul and this group of believers?

_____

_____

_____

♥ What two things did Paul and his companions share with the church there?

_____

_____

_____

♥ How is sharing the gospel closely connected with sharing life?

_____

_____

_____

_____

♥ What adjective is used to describe how Paul and his fellow workers felt about sharing the gospel as well as their very lives? Compare 1 Thessalonians

2:7–8 in at least four Bible versions and list the various adjectives below. (A great online source for doing this is biblegateway.com.)

_____

_____

_____

♥ Why does this passage say that Paul was "delighted" to share his very life with these brothers and sisters? When you love someone, are you purposeful to let them know that spending time with them is a pleasure rather than an obligation?

_____

_____

_____

♥ Think about your own life for a moment. Is there someone you recall who "delighted to share" his or her very life with you? What did they do? How does their example inspire you to do the same for others?

_____

_____

_____

Take inventory of recent conversations with those in your life, whether close friends and family members or perhaps just an acquaintance or coworker. Has someone been giving you heart drops? If so, who? Now prayerfully consider how you might encourage that person. Could you phone them? Text them a Bible verse? Write them a note and drop it in the mail? People need to know that others care. Let's not become so busy that we turn a deaf ear to the heart drops around us. Who might the Lord be calling you to encourage today?

LISTEN, LOVE, REPEAT, PAGE 73

3. In chapter four of *Listen, Love, Repeat*, Karen warns that noticing the necessary people in our lives isn't just a hobby. It isn't just something we engage in so we can snap a picture, upload it on social media, and then be elected humanitarian of the year. We don't do it to boast. Or to get a blessing in return. We show love to the necessary people in our lives because when we do, we are acknowledging that all humans are created in the image of God. Read Genesis 1:27 and then copy the verse below in your own handwriting. Circle the repeated phrase that tells how God made humans. Why is this important to remember when interacting with others?

_____

_____

_____

_____

Every day and every week, our lives naturally intersect with many people, all of whom bear the image of God. When we look beyond ourselves—and beyond the flaws and quirks of others—we see God. Is there someone in your life for whom you find it easy to notice their flaws and quirks but more difficult to see God's image in them? Jot your thoughts about it here.

_____

_____

_____

_____

Then, copy this sentence, filling in that person's name in the blank:

"_____ is wonderfully made in the image of God and I will remember that each time I see or speak to them."

4. In chapter four of *Keep It Shut*, Karen tells about her middle-school son—who sometimes pulled pranks at school and got in trouble—one day being praised by a food service employee for his respectful language and habit of calling his elders "ma'am" and "sir." Read 1 Peter 2:17. Then, answer the following questions:

♥ *Respect* is a verb—an action word. What two other action words also are mentioned in this verse, both in relation to how we treat others?

_____

_____

_____

♥ List all the individuals and groups of people mentioned in this verse along with the verb associated with them. (Hint: there are four people or groups and four corresponding verbs.)

_____

_____

_____

♥ We are called in this verse to "respect everyone." Is there someone for whom you find it difficult to respect? Why?

_____

_____

_____

♥ How can you still show them respect even when you do not approve of their behavior?

_____

_____

_____

5. On pages 97–98 of *Listen, Love, Repeat*, Karen writes, "By drawing on the power of the Holy Spirit to temper our tongues and guide our actions, we can speak politely and behave in a way that honors the image of God in each person we meet. This doesn't mean we don't occasionally speak hard truth. It just means we do so in an honorable way."

In the spaces below, take a couple of tries at speaking a hard truth but wording it in a civil and honorable (rather than a snippy and snarky) way. You may use real-life situations or just invent two scenarios for the sake of practice. An example is provided.

EXAMPLE

The person: Your combative neighbor who criticizes your decision to put a basketball hoop in your driveway because he's afraid the noise of your kids playing will bother him.

The words: "Thanks so much for feeling comfortable enough to voice your concerns with us. I can assure you the kids won't be playing after bedtime or at the crack of dawn so as to wake anyone who might be sleeping. But we are grateful that they love getting outside for fresh air and exercise, and this hoop will bring them—and the other neighborhood kids—lots of joy. I'm sure you remember playing outside with your friends when you were their age, don't you?"

The person:

_____

_____

The words:

_____

_____

_____

The person:

_____

_____

The words:

_____

_____

_____

6. In your Bible—or an online Scripture site such at biblegateway.com—look up the following verses that tell us how we are to treat one another. After carefully reading each verse, take a few moments to write out a summarizing statement that encompasses the commands in the verse in an easy-to-remember way.

♥ Galatians 5:13

_____

_____

♥ Ephesians 4:2

_____

_____

♥ 1 Peter 1:22

_____

_____

♥ John 15:12

_____

_____

♥ Romans 13:9

_____

_____

> We need to remember our *why*: the reason we love and serve and give thoughtful gifts and do good works. It is so that others will see Jesus. They may *look* at us, but we hope they *see* him.
>
> LISTEN, LOVE, REPEAT, PAGE 98

7. Take a few moments to think about your schedule. Do you have wiggle room in it for those times when you feel God nudging you to pick up the phone to call a hurting friend to see how he or she is doing? Is your life so jam-packed with activity that you can't ever seem to find time to take a meal to a grieving family or the one that just welcomed a new baby into their home? Reflect about whether there are any responsibilities you need to bow out of in order to have time to listen and love. We can't share life with others when we have the very life drained right out of us due to overcommitment. Note your reflections below as well as any action steps you can think of.

_____

_____

_____

_____

Write a two-or three-sentence prayer to God about this topic. Openly pour your heart out to him, asking the Holy Spirit to guide and empower you to make any changes needed.

_____

_____

_____

_____

Scripture Memory Verse of the Week Reminder

Keeping working on your week two Scripture memory verse! (See page 44.)

When You Live a Life of Welcome

Offer hospitality to one another without grumbling. Each of you should use whatever gift you have received to serve others, as faithful stewards of God's grace in its various forms.

(1 PETER 4: 9–10)

—————— Checking In (10 minutes) ——————

Welcome to session three of *Listen, Love, Repeat*. An important part of this study is sharing what you have learned from reading the book and from completing your between-sessions personal study. Remember, don't worry if you didn't get through all the material. You are still welcome at the study, and your input is valuable!

♥ What from the session two video segment most challenged or encouraged you since the group last met?

_____

_____

_____

_____

♥ What insights did you discover by reading chapters 3–4 of the *Listen, Love, Repeat* book? Share any particular favorites with the group.

_____

_____

_____

_____

♥ What did you find interesting or challenging in the between-sessions personal study questions?

_____

_____

_____

_____

♥ Do you have anything to report to the group concerning last session's challenge to "Make their day"? What necessary person did you choose to bless, and what did you do for them? How did they respond?

_____

_____

_____

_____

—— Video: When You Live a Life of Welcome (22 minutes) ——

Play the video segment for session three. As you watch, record any thoughts or concepts that stand out to you in the outline that follows.

NOTES

Living a life of welcome—opening both your heart and your home—means your stuff gets used. And reused. Over and over again.

_____

_____

_____

_____

Well-used items often mean that we have loved well.

_____

_____

_____

_____

Who really owns our stuff? First Chronicles 29:10–17 contains this sentiment spoken by King David: *Everything comes from you, and we have given you only what comes from your hand.* What an amazing perspective on our possessions.

_____

_____

_____

_____

When we have the mind-set that David has as he prays to God in front of the assembly, it makes it easier when our stuff gets stained. When our trinkets get tarnished. When our belongings get broken. After all, they belong to God.

_____

_____

_____

_____

Haven: a place of respite, retreat or refuge. In nautical terms—a place to drop anchor.

_____

_____

_____

_____

When we willingly open our homes, we aren't just being nice. We are being obedient to Scripture. (See 1 Peter 4:8–11.)

_____

_____

_____

_____

The Greek word for *hospitality* is a combination of two words: *love* and *guests*.

_____

_____

_____

_____

"Entertaining" puts the emphasis on you and impressing people. "Offering hospitality" puts the emphasis on loving your guests so that they feel refreshed—not impressed—when they leave your home. "Offer hospitality" is written as a command, not a suggestion.

_____

_____

_____

_____

Grumbling in the Greek means to murmur or whisper. Literally it means "smoldering discontent."

_____

_____

_____

_____

If there is room in your heart, somehow you can find room in your home.

_____

_____

_____

_____

Tips for opening both your heart and your home:

♥ Prepare your heart.

♥ Prepare your home.

♥ Stock the pantry.

♥ Listen, but refrain from preaching.

♥ Perfect the art of follow-up.

_____

_____

_____

_____

The first believers in the early church set a wonderful standard for us to follow. Acts 4:32 states, "No one claimed that any of their possessions was their own, but they shared everything they had."

_____

_____

_____

_____

First Peter 4:10 says, "Each of you should use whatever gift you have received to serve others, as faithful stewards of God's grace in its various forms."

_____

_____

_____

_____

———————— Group Discussion (10 minutes) ————————

Take a few minutes to discuss what you just watched.

1. What part of the video teaching had the most impact on you?

   _____

   _____

   _____

   _____

2. What has been your experience with hospitality? Has it been something you've enjoyed doing? Dreaded doing? Never done at all?

   _____

   _____

   _____

   _____

3. What part, if any, do social media sites like Pinterest or Instagram play in making us hesitant to open our homes to others?

   _____

   _____

   _____

   _____

4. Have someone read 1 Chronicles 29:10–17 aloud. Then answer the following questions based on the passage:

   ♥ What material items listed here are ones God owns?

   _____

   _____

   _____

   _____

♥ What other things does God possess that are not material items but qualities?

_____

_____

♥ Which verses talk about what our attitude should be toward material possessions and what phrases are used to describe how we should think about the things that we "own"?

_____

_____

_____

♥ Why do you think David spoke about this publicly, rather than privately to God? How might his perspective have challenged others to follow suit and adopt the attitude that everything belongs to God?

_____

_____

_____

♥ How does studying this passage challenge your own viewpoint when it comes to ownership and giving back to God?

_____

_____

_____

5. When we have a God-honoring perspective about our possessions and resources—even about our very lives—our hearts and homes can become a wheelhouse for ministry. On a scale from 1 to 10—with 1 being extremely hesitant and 10 being totally willing—how would you rate yourself when it comes to sharing your stuff, especially your home, with others? Why?

_____

_____

_____

──────── Cluster Group Discussion (12 minutes) ────────

If your group is comprised of more than twelve members, consider completing this discussion in smaller groups of three to six people each.

6. Have someone read 1 Peter 4:8–11 to your group. Then, answer the following:

    ♥ Are the commands in verses 8 and 9 connected? If so, how?

    _____

    _____

    _____

    ♥ Verse 10 urges us to use our gifts to serve others "as faithful stewards of God's grace in its various forms." How does using our gifts to serve others showcase God's grace?

    _____

    _____

    _____

    ♥ Verse 11 offers an important perspective for serving. We do it on God's behalf and in his strength. How does this challenge or motivate you?

    _____

    _____

    _____

    ♥ Verse 11 also mentions God being praised and given glory. The concept of glorifying God in the Scriptures literally means "to make him famous." How can having a biblical mind-set on hospitality–opening both our hearts and our homes–praise God and bring him glory (fame)?

    _____

    _____

    _____

♥ Can you think of an example of someone who offered hospitality in a loving manner, without grumbling, and in a way that made God known to others? Share your example with the group.

_____

_____

_____

_____

♥ When it comes to offering hospitality, we often can invent dozens of excuses for why we don't open our homes—it isn't large enough, or we aren't a gourmet cook, etc. . . . List as many excuses as you can for not opening your home to others. Have one member of your group record these excuses.

_____

_____

_____

_____

—————————— Group Discussion (10 minutes) ——————————

Gather back together as one large group and answer the following questions.

7. Verbally list the various the excuses for not offering hospitality, allowing each cluster group to report its findings.

_____

_____

_____

Now, how can what we learned from the 1 Peter 4:8–11 passage help each of us to dispel these excuses?

_____

_____

_____

8. *Grumbling* in the Greek means "to murmur or whisper." Literally it means "smoldering discontent." How does this word picture convict, challenge, or inspire you on the topic of hospitality?

_____

_____

_____

_____

9. *Haven* is defined as a place of respite, retreat, or refuge. In nautical terms, it's a place to drop anchor. What are some actions we can take to make our home a safe refuge and welcome retreat from the world for our family members—a place where others can be anchored in God's love? And how can we also make it such a place for those who are not our family members?

_____

_____

_____

_____

10. BONUS QUESTION: Have someone read 1 Timothy 6:17–19. Then answer the questions below.

   ♥ This verse starts out talking to those who are rich in this world. Does that only apply to millionaires or those who can afford a second home or brand new car? Think of everyone in the entire world. By comparison, are you "rich"?

   _____

   _____

   _____

   _____

   ♥ What are the rich told to do—and not to do—in this passage? List these actions below:

   We are told *not* to: _____

   We are told to: _____

♥ What do you think the final part of verse 19 means—"so that they may take hold of the life that is truly life"? If we have the proper perspective on our wealth and possessions, how can we really live the life God desires—not one of our own making?

_____

_____

_____

_____

11. BONUS QUESTION: Sometimes when we open our home to strangers, something exciting may be happening. Have someone in the group read Hebrews 13:2.

Now, if you *really* knew that angels were coming to your house, what would you feed them? Certainly not deviled eggs!;-) Have fun with your answers.

_____

_____

_____

_____

— Individual Activity: What Is God Asking Me to Do? (3 minutes) —

Complete this activity on your own.

Spend a few moments in prayer asking God to convict you of any wrong thoughts or attitudes about who owns your stuff, or about opening your home to others willingly. Then write a one-sentence goal going forward regarding either your attitude toward your possessions or your practice of opening your heart and home to others.

MY GOAL:

_____

_____

_____

_____

──────── Session 3 Memory Verse (1 minute) ────────

As a group, read aloud this session's memory verse:

> Offer hospitality to one another without grumbling. Each of you should use whatever gift you have received to serve others, as faithful stewards of God's grace in its various forms.
>
> (1 PETER 4: 9–10)

──────── Challenge Reminder and Closing Prayer (3 minutes) ────────

CHALLENGE: This week's challenge is to "Share your stuff." This may mean opening your home to someone, hosting a meal, or using your car to take someone out to lunch. Remember, everything we own comes from God! Our things are his, and he wants us to share them. Begin to think of what you might do to share your stuff this week.

PRAYER: Have one person close the session in prayer, focusing on remembering that God really owns our stuff and we make him famous when we willingly share our possessions and homes with others. Don't forget to follow through on your one-sentence goal from your individual activity. Then, get ready for your between-sessions personal study prior to session four.

Between-Sessions Personal Study

SESSION 3

Challenge Reminder

This week's challenge is to "Share your stuff." This may mean opening your home to someone, hosting a meal, or using your car to take someone out to lunch. Remember, everything we own comes from God! Our things are his, and he wants us to share them. Begin to think of what you might do to share your stuff this week. Then put it on the schedule and follow through!

Session 3 Memory Verse

Below is the memory verse for this session. Write it on a notecard or type it in the notes app on your phone. Remember, all the memory verses are printed together at the back of this study guide on pages 157–158. You may photocopy them for your convenience. Set an alarm for at least two times a day when you know you will have a minute to look over this week's verse and commit it to memory.

[
Offer hospitality to one another without grumbling. Each of you should use whatever gift you have received to serve others, as faithful stewards of God's grace in its various forms.
]

(1 PETER 4: 9–10)

Read and Learn

Read chapters 5–6 of the *Listen, Love, Repeat* book. Use the space below to record any insights you discovered, concepts that challenged you, or questions you may want to bring to the next group session.

_____

_____

_____

_____

_____

Study and Reflect

1. In chapter 5 of *Listen, Love, Repeat*, Karen notes that Romans 12:15 commands to us to help ease the suffering of others: "Rejoice with those who rejoice; weep with those who weep" (ESV). Can you think of a time when someone shared in either your joy or your suffering in a way that was meaningful and made a lasting impact? Briefly describe it here.

    _____

    _____

    _____

    _____

2. Read chapter one of the book of Ruth. Then, answer this question: What about Ruth's behavior toward her grieving mother-in-law most inspires, motivates, or challenges you when it comes to walking alongside someone who is hurting? (You can also look over the summary points found on pages 116–119 of the book *Listen, Love, Repeat* to see if any of those resonate with you.)

    _____

    _____

    _____

    _____

As we go through life this week, may we be ever aware of those around us who are grieving—for a friend, a loved one, a marriage, a job, or a relationship. May we seek to weep with them, reaching out to help carry their load. When we do, we fulfill the law of Christ.

Whose load will you help carry this week?

Listen, Love, Repeat, page 121

3. For each of the following pairs of statements, circle the one that best describes your current actions and attitudes about encouraging the sorrowful, sharing your possessions, and opening your heart and home to whomever God brings your way. Or, if you are somewhere in between place an X between the statements.

I steer clear of those who are grieving and sorrowful.	I gravitate toward those who are dealing with grief and loss.
I have never really thought much about the fact that it is really God who owns all of my possessions.	I recognize that all I have actually belongs to God himself and not to me personally.
Rarely do I think of inviting others over to my home.	I often have people over for a visit or even a meal.
I've never really put much effort into making my home a haven of rest and retreat.	I intentionally try to make my home a welcoming place for my family and friends.
I haven't ever connected my house and my belongings with ministry before.	I always view my home and my possessions as tools for reaching others for Christ.

4. While speaking of 1 Chronicles 29:10–17 in the teaching, Karen posed this question: If the ancient Israelites were so willing to offer up what God had given them, turning right back around and investing in building his temple, could we today use all that he has given us to build up fellow believers and encourage others who might not know him yet? It is a subtle but crucial shift in perspective when we realize that all the material items we have worked for here on Earth really do not belong to us. Instead they all come from the hand of God.

Are there any of your possessions of which you are quite protective and have a hard time sharing with others? If so, list them.

_____

_____

_____

_____

Why do you feel you have a difficult time sharing this item (or items) with others? Did it cost a lot of money? Are you afraid it will get damaged?

_____

_____

_____

_____

Do you need to make an attitude adjustment about the item or items you listed? If so, write out a short prayer about it below.

_____

_____

_____

_____

It is a subtle but crucial shift in perspective when we realize that all the material items we have worked for here on Earth really do not belong to us. Instead they all come from the hand of God. They are his in the first place, and they are his at the end of our lives. The question comes down to this: who owns your stuff?

Listen, Love, Repeat, page 130

5. In the video, Karen taught about the deeper meaning of 1 Peter 4:9: "Offer hospitality to one another without grumbling." She mentioned that this is a command, not just a suggestion. What does it mean to you that God doesn't just encourage us to offer hospitality but actually *expects* us to provide it?

_____

_____

_____

_____

     Karen also taught us that the word *grumbling* in the Greek means to murmur or whisper. Literally it means "smoldering discontent." In other words, it isn't necessarily audible. Instead it refers to complaining secretly in our hearts and minds. When a fire is smoldering, the flame isn't readily visible to others but rather somewhat hidden. However, a smoldering fire can still do horrific damage. How might our hidden-but-still-horrific attitude of grumbling damage or hinder the cause of bringing glory to God and advancing his kingdom here on Earth?

_____

_____

_____

_____

6. Think back to your group study time for this session. List some excuses below for not opening your home to others. (If you missed this session's group time, come up with your own excuses.)

_____

_____

_____

_____

    Which of these excuses have you ever used in the past? Are you using any of them today? How does learning the fact that opening our homes isn't just a nice idea but a scriptural command prompt you to stop using this excuse?

_____

_____

_____

_____

7. Karen gave the following practical tips for opening our hearts and homes to others. Draw a circle in front of the one that comes the easiest for you. Draw a square in front of the one that is the most challenging. Finally, draw a star in front of the one you'd most like to try to implement in the near future.

> Prepare your heart.
>
> Prepare your home.
>
> Stock the pantry.
>
> Listen, but refrain from preaching.
>
> Perfect the art of follow-up.

8. The definition of *haven* is a place of respite, retreat, and refuge. In nautical terms, it's a place to drop anchor. Think of the people in your life today. Would they say that your home is a safe place—a haven for them when they are stressed or troubled? Why or why not?

_____

_____

_____

_____

In the space below write one action step you can take in the next week or two to make your place more inviting or to alert others to the fact that your home is open should they want to utilize it as a respite from the world for a while.

_____

_____

_____

_____

Scripture Memory Verse of the Week Reminder

How's your work coming along on this week's memory verse (see page 66)? Can you still recite the verses for sessions one and two?

How to Hug a Porcupine and Squeeze a Skunk

The King will reply, "Truly I tell you, whatever you did for one of the least of these brothers and sisters of mine, you did for me."

(MATTHEW 25:40)

──────── **Checking In (10 minutes)** ────────

Welcome to session four of *Listen, Love, Repeat*. An important part of this study is sharing what you have learned from reading the book and from completing your between-sessions personal study. Remember, don't worry if you didn't get through all the material. You are still welcome at the study, and your input is valuable!

♥ What from the session three video teaching most challenged or encouraged you since the group last met?

_____

_____

_____

_____

♥ What insights did you discover from reading chapters 5–6 of the *Listen, Love, Repeat* book?

_____

_____

_____

_____

♥ What most spoke to you from the between-sessions personal study questions?

_____

_____

_____

_____

♥ Do you have anything to report to the group concerning last session's challenge to "Share your stuff"? What did you do to either use one of your possessions to bless someone else or to open your home willingly–and *without* grumbling to yourself about it?

_____

_____

_____

_____

Play the video segment for session four. As you watch, record any thoughts or concepts that stand out to you in the outline that follows.

NOTES

In the story of Rudy with the Cooties, God challenged Karen to see beyond the weird and find something wonderful instead.

_____

_____

_____

_____

Tucked in the book of Psalms we read a simple but powerful verse, Psalm 68:6: "God sets the lonely in families."

_____

_____

_____

God's plan all along was that we would do life in community. We are meant to live out our great vertical fellowship with God through horizontal connections with our fellow humans. We see this concept throughout Scripture.

_____

_____

_____

In Genesis 2:18 we read what God declared after creating Adam: "It is not good for the man to be alone."

_____

_____

_____

_____

In the New Testament, Jesus himself modeled this principle when he sent out the disciples not as a solo act but in pairs to spread the good news of the kingdom (see Luke 10:1).

_____

_____

_____

_____

"Do you not know that God entrusted you with that money (all above what buys necessities for your families) to feed the hungry, to clothe the naked, to help the stranger, the widow, the fatherless; and, indeed, as far as it will go, to relieve the wants of all mankind? How *can* you, how *dare* you, defraud the Lord, by applying it to any other purpose?"–eighteenth-century preacher John Wesley

_____

_____

_____

_____

So who are the lonely, left out, and unloved, and why should we seek them out? Jesus gives us a clue in Luke 14:12–14: the poor, the marginalized, the lonely, and those who can never repay you.

_____

_____

_____

_____

Most foreign exchange students are in the US for four years or more, but almost 90 percent of them never see the inside of an American home.

_____

_____

_____

_____

In the eyes of those society forgets, we can see the presence of our Savior. When we do it for the "least of these," we do it for Christ (see Matthew 25:31–40).

_____

_____

_____

_____

But sometimes, the "least of these" aren't timid and shy and sweet–they can be larger-than-life scary too! We need to learn to hug a porcupine and squeeze a skunk.

_____

_____

_____

_____

How many big bad people–just like Karen's former student John–might have their icy cold hearts melted by a little dose of undeserving love?

_____

_____

_____

_____

Throughout the New Testament, we see Jesus spending his time on Earth with the not-so-popular people. He modeled for us upside-down living and loving.

_____

_____

_____

_____

Second Corinthians 1:3–4 says, "Praise be to the God and Father of our Lord Jesus Christ, the Father of compassion and the God of all comfort, who comforts us in all our troubles, so that we can comfort those in any trouble with the comfort we ourselves receive from God."

_____

_____

_____

_____

──────────── **Group Discussion (10 minutes)** ────────────

Take a few minutes to discuss what you just watched.

1. What part of the teaching had the most impact on you?

_____

_____

_____

_____

2. Do you know of any stories similar to the one about Rudy with the Cooties or Big Bad John that happened either to you or to someone you know? Share it with the group.

_____

_____

_____

3. Psalm 68:6 declares, "God sets the lonely in families." Have you ever witnessed this happening—either to you as the lonely one or to someone else who needed to feel loved, wanted, and included? Tell what happened.

_____

_____

_____

_____

"If you want to know what's really inside a person, listen carefully to the words she speaks."

LYSA TERKEURST, *UNINVITED*, PAGE 4

──────── **Cluster Group Discussion (12 minutes)** ────────

If your group is comprised of more than twelve members, consider completing this discussion in smaller groups of three to six people each.

4. Have a person read aloud the following passages one at a time. After each is read, discuss what you learned about how God treats others—or about how *we* are supposed to treat them. Record your findings in the spaces provided:

♥ Psalm 12:5

_____

_____

♥ Psalm 34:6

_____

_____

♥ Psalm 34:18

_____

_____

♥ Psalm 41:3

_____

_____

♥ Luke 6:35–36

_____

_____

♥ Luke 6:37

_____

_____

♥ 1 Thessalonians 5:14

_____

_____

5. Which of the preceding passages most challenged or convicted you? Can you share the reason why?

_____

_____

_____

_____

If you were going to pick one of these passages to memorize, which one would it be and why?

_____

_____

_____

_____

For the brave and ambitious: Exchange cell phone numbers with someone else in your group who might also want to memorize one of the passages. Text each other throughout the week to see how your memorization is coming or even to talk on the phone and practice together. Then, next week when you get together, before or after class, try to recite the passage from memory with your study partner.

──────────── Group Discussion (5 minutes) ────────────

Gather back together as one large group and answer the following questions.

6. Have the cluster groups take turns summarizing what they discovered from the Bible passages about how God treats people and how we should treat others as well. How many in the group decided to take on the memory verse challenge with a partner?

_____

_____

_____

_____

7. In the video session, Karen read the words of the eighteenth-century preacher John Wesley:

> Do you not know that God entrusted you with that money (all above what buys necessities for your families) to feed the hungry, to clothe the naked, to help the stranger, the widow, the fatherless; and, indeed, as far as it will go, to relieve the wants of all mankind? How *can* you, how *dare* you, defraud the Lord, by applying it to any other purpose?

What do you think of this perspective? Do you agree or disagree with it? Have you ever thought of using money for yourself beyond what you and your family really needs as "defrauding the Lord"?

_____

_____

_____

_____

How does this quote puzzle, challenge, or convict you? Or, do you not agree with what it says? If you were to take Wesley's advice and use your excess money for another cause, which one would it be from the ones listed in the quote—the hungry, the naked, the stranger, the widow, or the fatherless? Can you think of a modern-day organization you would give the money to that ministers to one of the categories mentioned?

_____

_____

_____

_____

8. BONUS QUESTION: Jesus talked a great deal about money and the poor. Have someone read aloud Luke 12:32–34. Then answer the questions below:

♥ Be honest. What runs through your mind when you read that Jesus urged selling our possessions and giving the proceeds to the poor? Do you think, "But I worked for my possessions!"? Or, "If people were not lazy, then they might not be poor"? How do Jesus' words sit with you?

_____

_____

_____

_____

♥ Do you think that Jesus means we need to sell all of our possessions and give the money away? Could he instead be referring to a heart issue—that we often care more about ourselves and our wealth than about the less fortunate and their plight? How does verse 34 fit with this notion?

_____

_____

_____

_____

♥ Does the Bible teach that those of us who have money need to take care of people who do not have a job and therefore are poor? Or, is there a distinction made in Scripture? Have someone read aloud 2 Thessalonians 3:9–10 and then discuss this concept. What does the end of verse 10 *not* say?

_____

_____

_____

_____

9. BONUS QUESTION: Karen once had a college sociology professor who gave over 40 percent of his income away to the poor and needy and lived on the remaining 60 percent in a small, humble house. He wore the same two or three

sweaters over and over. He drove a clunker of a car. He felt personally convicted that he should not have so much money, while others were struggling to put groceries on the table. Have you ever known someone who lives on very little in order to give more money away to the poor, charities, or other humanitarian causes? How has their example inspired you?

_____

_____

_____

_____

— Individual Activity: What Is God Asking Me to Do? (5 minutes) —

Ask God to bring to mind a person in your life who is either lonely, someone society deems as less-than-lovely, or even hard-to-love. Write their name on the line below.

_____

Now, write a prayer—speaking to God with all honesty—about this person. Ask God to bless them and to soften your heart toward them and to be loving and kind when you interact with them in the future. Also, list a few possible ideas for how you might show them love.

My prayer:

_____

_____

_____

My ideas:

_____

_____

_____

—————— **Session 4 Memory Verse (1 minute)** ——————

As a group, read aloud this session's memory verse:

> The King will reply, "Truly I tell you, whatever you did for one of the least of these brothers and sisters of mine, you did for me."
>
> (MATTHEW 25:40)

—————— **Challenge Reminder and Closing Prayer (2 minutes)** ——————

CHALLENGE: This session's challenge will get you out of your comfort zone by lifting up a lonely, hugging a porcupine, or squeezing a skunk. Pick one person who is difficult for you to reach out to because of his or her circumstance or who is just plain hard to love! Do one thing to show that person God's unconditional love in a tangible way.

PRAYER: Have one person close the session in prayer, focusing on the lonely, less-than-lovely, and hard-to-love. Then, get ready for your between-sessions personal study time prior to the next meeting.

Between-Sessions Personal Study

SESSION 4

Challenge Reminder

This session's challenge will get you out of your comfort zone by lifting up a lonely, hugging a porcupine, or squeezing a skunk. Pick one person who is difficult for you to reach out to because of his or her circumstance or who is just plain hard to love! Do one thing to show that person God's unconditional love in a tangible way. Who knows? You may just melt an icy heart with a lavish dose of undeserved love.

Session 4 Memory Verse

Below is the memory verse for this session. Write it on a notecard, type it in the notes app on your phone, or photocopy the designed one from page 158. Set an alarm for at least two times a day when you know you will have a minute to look over the verse and commit it to memory.

> The King will reply, "Truly I tell you, whatever you did for one of the least of these brothers and sisters of mine, you did for me."
>
> (MATTHEW 25:40)

Read and Learn

Read chapters 7–8 of the *Listen, Love, Repeat* book. Use the space below to record any insights you discovered or questions you may want to bring to the next group session.

_____

_____

_____

_____

_____

_____

Study and Reflect

1. In session four, Karen told several stories about people she met: Rudy with the Cooties–the neighborhood boy who sold her own rocks to her, Big Bad

John—the tough middle school teen who needed a little love and attention, Shu—the foreign exchange student from China who was going to be all alone Thanksgiving break, and "Big Bubba"—the teenager who, when he thought about home, thought of Karen's house. Which of these stories most resonated with you or inspired you to reach out to someone in need of love and attention?

_____

_____

_____

_____

Why did you choose that particular story? Did you see yourself in it? Did it remind you of someone in your own life? Did it give you any ideas for doing something similar for someone you know?

_____

_____

_____

_____

2. In chapter seven of the book *Listen, Love, Repeat*, Karen mentions that from the beginning of time, God's plan was that humanity would do life in community. He declared in the Old Testament that it was not good for man to be alone. In the New Testament, Jesus sent out the disciples in pairs. What other Bible stories or verses can you think of that show God wants us to live in community, supporting and encouraging each other rather than going it alone? You may search online at biblegateway.com, using key words such as *alone*, *friends*, and *one another*.

_____

_____

_____

_____

> God certainly has the means to comfort the afflicted (and per-
> haps afflict the comfortable, who might see such reaching out as
> being *waaaaay* out of their comfort zone!), but he chooses to work
> through us and through our families. He draws others to himself
> through our voices, our food, our love, and our lives.
>
> LISTEN, LOVE, REPEAT, PAGE 151

3. In chapter seven of *Listen, Love, Repeat* (pages 157–158), Karen talks about how when we reach out to those who are marginalized, poor, misfits, or hard-to-love, we might think we are doing it for them, but in reality someone else is the recipient of our actions–the Lord himself. Read Matthew 25:31–40 and then write a short prayer reminder about this concept in the space below, using specific people in your own life. EXAMPLE: *Father, help me to remember that when I encounter the mentally challenged man at church who wants to talk to me for a long time each Sunday when I'd rather be visiting with my friend, as I stop to show him love and attention, I am doing it for you.*

_____

_____

_____

_____

4. Take a few moments to read Luke 6:27–36 printed on the next page. As you do, mark it in the following way:

   ♥ Circle any phrases that tell what unkind or evil actions others may take toward us.

   ♥ Draw a box around any references to how we are commanded to behave.

   ♥ Place a star next to any verses that reference God's actions or character.

   ♥ Finally, go back and put a ☺ next to your favorite verse or section of this passage.

   ♥ (NOTE: You may also use three different colored highlighters for the three different marks and a ☺ for your favorite verse.)

After you have finished: What has this little markup exercise taught you? What principles can you draw from Luke 6:27–36 that will help you in your interactions with those who may not treat you well?

_____

_____

_____

_____

LUKE 6:27–36

27 "But to you who are listening I say: Love your enemies, do good to those who hate you,

28 bless those who curse you, pray for those who mistreat you.

29 If someone slaps you on one cheek, turn to them the other also. If someone takes your coat, do not withhold your shirt from them.

30 Give to everyone who asks you, and if anyone takes what belongs to you, do not demand it back.

31 Do to others as you would have them do to you.

32 If you love those who love you, what credit is that to you? Even sinners love those who love them.

33 And if you do good to those who are good to you, what credit is that to you? Even sinners do that.

34 And if you lend to those from whom you expect repayment, what credit is that to you? Even sinners lend to sinners, expecting to be repaid in full.

35 But love your enemies, do good to them, and lend to them without expecting to get anything back. Then your reward will be great, and you will be children of the Most High, because he is kind to the ungrateful and wicked.

36 Be merciful, just as your Father is merciful."

> In addition to loving people who were socially marginalized, Jesus loved those who hated and despised him. Those who treated him terribly. He encouraged his followers to do the same, without excuse.
>
> *LISTEN, LOVE, REPEAT, PAGE 174*

5. When dealing with others who are regarded as less fortunate or looked down on by society, we must remember to not become proud or arrogant. Luke 14:11 can help us to keep a God-honoring attitude. Look up this verse and then write it out below in your own sweet handwriting:

_____

_____

_____

_____

In chapter 8 of *Listen, Love, Repeat* (pages 175–176), Karen writes:

> *Within the faces of the unlovely and hard-to-love, we must see ourselves. We must recognize that we too, at our very core, are unlovable as well. We are not perfect. We sin. We hate. We have cruel thoughts occasionally and sometimes display cruel actions. Because God showed us great mercy and kindness, overlooking our faults and forgiving our sins through his Son's shed blood on the cross, we in turn need to show mercy and kindness to those who seem hard to love. It begins with humility.*

What do you think of this standpoint—seeing ourselves within the faces of the unlovely and hard-to-love? Is it something you have thought about before or not?

_____

_____

_____

_____

When dealing with a difficult person, what can you say to yourself—not out loud but in your mind—to help you to practice patience, display grace, and show forgiveness? Write what you will say to yourself here:

_____
_____
_____
_____

> When we do good to those who would seek to harm us, or show love to those who mistreat or talk badly about us, we are modeling Jesus' behavior. He was merciful, just as God our Father is merciful. It is a countercultural idea to love the unloving. But it is God's plan for us.
>
> *Listen, Love, Repeat*, page 175

6. Look up 2 Corinthians 1:3–4 and read it over a few times slowly, letting its message sink in. Then answer the following:

   ♥ What two titles are given to God in verse 3?

   _____
   _____

   ♥ What does verse 4 say he does?

   _____
   _____

   ♥ What are we then told we are empowered to do?

   _____
   _____
   _____

♥ Can you think of a time when you saw this play out in real life? Were you the one doing the comforting or were you being comforted by someone else?

_____

_____

_____

♥ How does this passage display the link between the hard times in our lives and God's purpose for us when it comes to relationships?

_____

_____

_____

7. Pages 177–181 of *Listen, Love, Repeat* includes seven pieces of advice for hugging a porcupine or squeezing a skunk. They are recorded below. Circle the one or two that you feel you most need to remember and work on when dealing with the hard-to-love in the future.

♥ Pray. Pray. And then pray some more.

♥ Go slow.

♥ Be curious.

♥ Serve.

♥ Keep showing up.

♥ Expect nothing in return. Zero. Zip. Nada.

♥ Glance at them, but fix your gaze on Jesus.

Now write a few words about why you circled that particular piece of advice:

_____

_____

_____

Scripture Memory Verse of the Week Reminder

Quick! Can you recite this week's memory verse? Take a peek on page 86 if you need to practice a few more times.

Family Matters

Be kind and compassionate to one another, forgiving each other, just as in Christ God forgave you.

(EPHESIANS 4:32)

—————————— Checking In (10 minutes) ——————————

Welcome to session five of *Listen, Love, Repeat*. An important part of this study is sharing what you have learned from reading the book and from completing your between-sessions personal study. Remember, you are still welcome at the study even if you weren't able to complete the material.

♥ Think back to the session four video segment. Is there anything that comes to your mind as memorable when you think of that video?

_____

_____

_____

♥ What insights did you discover from reading chapters 7–8 of the *Listen, Love, Repeat* book?

_____

_____

_____

♥ What most jumped out at you from the between-sessions personal study?

_____

_____

_____

♥ Last session's challenge was designed to get us out of our comfort zones by lifting up a lonely, hugging a porcupine, or squeezing a skunk. Does anyone have a story to share about this challenge to show God's love to someone who might be a little hard to love?

_____

_____

_____

—————— Video: Family Matters (23 minutes) ——————

Play the video segment for session five. As you watch, record any thoughts or concepts that stand out to you in the outline that follows.

NOTES

Late comedian George Burns once said, "Happiness is having a large, loving, caring, close-knit family . . . in another city."

_____

_____

_____

_____

Loving our families can be tricky—perhaps for two reasons:

♥ The folks we love the most are also the people who most drive us nuts!

♥ Secondly, because they are our relatives—our own flesh and blood or legally adopted and totally connected kin—they *have* to love us!

_____

_____

_____

_____

Ephesians 4:17–32 gives us many "dos" and "don'ts" of the faith. First we have the "don'ts":

♥ Don't be given to futile thinking (verse 17). In the Greek, this means "empty and purposeless reasoning." Such people let their minds wander and make up their own rules.

♥ Don't let your heart be hardened (verse 18). The Greek word here for "hardened" was used to describe solid marble used in construction, and it was also used medically to describe something that was numb or callused.

♥ Don't become impure and greedy (verse 19). In the Greek, *impure* referred to something that had a foreign matter mixed in and *greedy* meant "aggressively covetous."

_____

_____

_____

_____

Next, we have the "dos":

♥ Do put off your old, corrupt, deceitful self (verse 22). In the Greek, the phrase *put off* means to "renounce, lay aside, or stow away." *Corrupt* is best translated as "spoiled, rotten, and ruined." And *deceitful* means "falseness that is motivated by fraud." So, we are to reject our rotten, ruined, and totally fraudulent way of thinking—to take it off and stow it away far from us.

♥ Do put on a new mind and a new self (verse 24). The concept of having a new mind in the original Greek means a renewed way of thinking—one that is a stage higher and that, by God's power, intensifies more and more. And the new self means "fresh, novel, innovative, not ever found to exist before."

_____

_____

_____

_____

The big "do" of putting on the new self encompasses a lot of other smaller "dos." First, there are some things we must do with our mouths:

♥ Do speak truthfully to others (verse 25).

♥ Do deal with your anger promptly and not let it lead you to the point of sin where you give the devil a foothold (verse 26–27).

♥ Do talk in a wholesome way, building others up rather than tearing them down (verse 29).

♥ Do refrain from slandering another person or speaking with malice (verse 31). *Slander* in the Greek here means "scurrilous," which is defined as making or spreading scandalous claims about someone with the sole intention of damaging their reputation. And *malice* means speaking spitefully about someone in a nasty, hurtful, and revengeful way.

_____

_____

_____

_____

Besides our mouths there are also certain "dos" we must carry out with our minds and in our actions:

♥ Do get rid of bitterness, rage, anger, and brawling (verse 31).

♥ Do be kind, compassionate, and forgiving—just as God, through Jesus, forgave you. The word *compassionate* here literally means "tenderhearted" (verse 32).

_____

_____

_____

_____

When we follow the list of faith "dos" and "don'ts" in Ephesians 4, the result is that we please God and we don't grieve the Holy Spirit (verse 30). *Grieve* means "to inflict deep, severe, emotional pain."

_____

_____

_____

_____

We are sealed with the Holy Spirit. This language refers to a king's signet ring. He would use his signet ring to make an impression on something, showing that it either belonged to him or he approved of it.

_____

_____

_____

_____

Here are some practical ways to show love to your family:

♥ Eat together.

♥ Send group texts.

♥ Pray. And let them know you are praying.

♥ Adopt the practice of unbirthdays.

_____

_____

_____

_____

Somehow, forge a family. Take all the irregular people that bear your name and share your heritage. God will place them together in the most beautiful of ways.

_____

_____

_____

_____

Embracing our less-than-perfect families gives us a picture of how God embraces us.

_____

_____

_____

_____

───────── Group Discussion (10 minutes) ─────────

Take a few minutes to discuss what you just watched.

1. What part of the teaching had the most impact on you?

_____

_____

_____

2. Can you relate to the story of pulling out all the stops for others—making food for someone who needed encouragement or showing love to someone outside your four walls—while neglecting to do the same for your own family members? Have you ever done this or had it done to you? What happened?

_____

_____

_____

_____

_____

   Of the two reasons Karen gave why we might try harder to minister to others than to our own family, with which one do you struggle most and why?

   ♥ The folks we hold most dear can also be the people with whom we experience the greatest conflict.

   ♥ Secondly, because they are our relatives—our own flesh and blood or legally adopted and totally connected kin—they *have* to love us!

_____

_____

_____

_____

_____

3. Look up Ephesians 4:17–32 and take turns having members read these verses aloud. As the passage is read, note which "dos" or "don'ts" of the faith jump out at you. Is it because it's an issue with which you struggle? A behavior you have changed or an obstacle you have overcome? Something that you feel a tad bit convicted about? After the reading, take turns having members share with the group which "do" or "don't" stands out to them and why.

_____

_____

_____

_____

Look again at verses 20–24. What picture is painted here? How does this portion of Scripture give you inspiration or direction for dealing with the particular "do" or "don't" of the faith you chose?

_____

_____

_____

_____

─────── **Cluster Group Discussion (10 minutes)** ───────

If your group is comprised of more than twelve members, consider completing this discussion in smaller groups of three to six people each.

4. Have someone read aloud Colossians 3:12–14 as the rest of the group listens. After the passage is read, discuss how it applies to relationships in your immediate—or even extended—family.

_____

_____

_____

_____

Next, as a group, use the passage to find eight different actions or attitudes we are told to do or have. Record them in the space below.

♥ _____

♥ _____

♥ _____

♥ _____

♥ _____

♥ _____

♥ _____

♥ _____

This passage urges us to "clothe" ourselves with these various character qualities in verse 12. Then, in verse 14, we are urged to "put on" love, which binds all the virtues together in perfect unity. How does this image of clothing yourself speak to you? Why is love the virtue that holds them all together? Does this make you think of any other verses about love from Scripture?

_____

_____

_____

_____

———————————— Group Discussion (12 minutes) ————————————

Gather back together as one large group and answer the following questions.

5. Have the cluster groups each share one insight from their discussion of Colossians 3:12–14.

_____

_____

_____

_____

6. During the video session discussion of the "dos" and "don'ts" of the faith found in Ephesians 4, Karen noted verse 30 which reads: "And do not grieve the Holy Spirit of God, with whom you were sealed for the day of redemption."

    She mentioned that in the original Greek, *grieve* means "to inflict deep, severe, emotional pain." How does it make you feel knowing that this is how the Holy Spirit reacts when seeing us relating to others in an improper manner?

_____

_____

_____

_____

7. The final half of Ephesians 4:30 mentions that we are "sealed" with the Holy Spirit for the day of redemption. Karen shared that this language was used to describe a king who would use his signet ring to make an impression on something, showing that either he approved it or it belonged to him. Often this was done by melting wax and then pressing the king's ring into it. When dried, the wax affixed itself to the object and showed that the document or the item had

the full backing of the king. How does this help you to understand the Holy Spirit's role in the life of the Christian?

_____

_____

_____

_____

8. Karen urged each of us to somehow forge a family—taking all the irregular people that bear our name and share our heritage—and allow God to knit them together in the most beautiful of ways. Discuss this sentence: *Embracing your less-than-perfect family is a picture of how God embraces you.*

_____

_____

_____

_____

9. BONUS QUESTION: Look back at question 4 and the eight different actions or attitudes with which Colossians 3 commands us to clothe ourselves. Do these remind you of any other Scripture passage? Turn to Galatians 5:22–23 and then choose one person to read aloud these verses.

This passage lists nine characteristics of the Holy Spirit—what we commonly call the fruit of the Spirit. List them below:

♥ _____

♥ _____

♥ _____

♥ _____

♥ _____

♥ _____

♥ _____

♥ _____

Now, go back and compare these nine characteristics with the eight different actions or attitudes you found in Colossians 3. Circle any concepts of the nine listed above from Galatians 5 that are also mentioned in Colossians 3, or are at least somewhat similar.

10. BONUS QUESTION: Review all of the characteristics you recorded from both Colossians 3 and Galatians 5. For those who feel comfortable sharing, which of these characteristics is hardest for you to display with someone in your immediate or extended family? Don't use the person's name; just describe the situation. How might the truth of these passages help you when you interact with this person in the future? What will you say to yourself the next time a situation starts to get sticky or turn ugly?

_____

_____

_____

_____

— Individual Activity: What Is God Asking Me to Do? (3 minutes) —

Take a moment to get alone with your thoughts, quiet before the Lord. Ask him to reveal one area in your conduct toward a family member—or members—where you need to change. Is there someone you have a hard time being kind to because of how they treat you? Do you lack compassion for a particular relative? Are you harboring bitterness toward someone in the family who you just can't seem to forgive? Write what comes to mind here. (If you aren't experiencing such a situation at the moment, thank God and then spend this time praying for your fellow group members as they do this exercise.)

_____

_____

_____

_____

Now, in your own handwriting, copy the phrase on page 104 that is strategically stitched inside Ephesians 4:32, BUT don't put a period at the end of the sentence. Instead, add the words "even when it comes to" and then craft a phrase about the situation of which you just wrote to finish your sentence.

Be kind and compassionate to one another, forgiving each other, just as in Christ God forgave you, even when it comes to . . .

_____

_____

_____

_____

———————— Session 5 Memory Verse (1 minute) ————————

As a group, read aloud this session's memory verse:

> Be kind and compassionate to one another, forgiving each other, just as in Christ God forgave you.
>
> (EPHESIANS 4:32)

———— Challenge Reminder and Closing Prayer (2 minutes) ————

CHALLENGE: This week, focus on your family and detonate a love bomb. Choose one person to whom you are related and do something to show your love for them. It can be a simple gesture or a more elaborate action. Anything that will convey to them that you are crazy about them—even if they drive you crazy sometimes. And don't panic. Several ideas are provided in the between-sessions personal study.

PRAYER: Have one person close the session in prayer, keeping in mind the theme of loving our families, even the difficult members. The next time the group meets will be the final teaching segment. Booo!!! Are you already tearing up? Enjoy your study time between sessions.

Between-Sessions Personal Study

SESSION 5

IMPORTANT NOTE TO FACILITATORS
This study includes an *optional* seventh session wrap-up party. However, it is strongly recommended that you hold this session because it helps tie together and drive home the main point of the whole study. If you are a group facilitator, be sure to look over the bonus session material (pages 135–151) before session six, so that you can coordinate the details at the end of the meeting. This includes planning for food and theme.

Challenge Reminder

DETONATE A LOVE BOMB! This week you will focus on your family and detonate a love bomb. Choose one person to whom you are related and do something to show your love. It can be a simple gesture or a more elaborate action. And don't panic. Several ideas are provided at the end of this personal study section.

Below is the memory verse for this session. Write it on a notecard, type it in the notes app on your phone, or photocopy the version found on page 158. Set an alarm for at least two times a day when you know you will have a minute to look over the verse and commit it to memory.

> Be kind and compassionate to one another, forgiving each other, just as in Christ God forgave you.
>
> (EPHESIANS 4:32)

Read and Learn

Read chapter 9 of the *Listen, Love, Repeat* book and record any thoughts or insights you discovered in the space provided here.

_____

_____

_____

_____

_____

_____

The admonitions in the Bible about treating others well also apply to those who use the last drop of milk without telling us or who ruin our new white shirt by washing it with their new red sweatshirt. Yes, those who tick us off most are still people whom God calls us to love and serve and honor.

LISTEN, LOVE, REPEAT, PAGE 193

Study and Reflect

1. In chapter nine of *Listen, Love, Repeat* (pages 192–194), Karen writes about how we have trouble showing our relatives the same courtesy that we show non-family members. Take a moment to honestly reflect. Do your family members witness you treating others with more respect than you show them? Do you speak kindly and politely to those outside your family while hurling harsh words at your own people? Place an X on the continuum below to show where you currently rank on this relational issue.

I often speak to my family in a disrespectful or harsh manner.

I sometimes speak to my family in an impolite or unkind way.

I rarely have trouble speaking to my family respectfully and with consideration.

Why did you place your X on the spot you chose? Are you satisfied with where you currently stand on this matter? How would you like to see progress in this area? Be specific and compose a few sentences below with your behavior-altering goal.

_____

_____

_____

As mentioned in this session's video segment, we can either have hard hearts or tender hearts. Our session memory verse, Ephesians 4:32, is quoted in the NIV translation. However, for the moment, let's consider the *Amplified Bible* translation, which offers some additional insight.

> Be kind *and* helpful to one another, tender-hearted [compassionate, understanding], forgiving one another [readily and freely], just as God in Christ also forgave you (AMP).

Look at the verse closely again. Circle any word or phrase that seems to resonate with you when you think about how you should be treating your family members.

Keeping the *Amplified Bible* version of this verse in mind, what little pep talk can you give yourself about how you need to be more tenderhearted–rather than hard-hearted–when dealing with certain family members' personalities or habits? Write your thoughts here.

_____

_____

_____

_____

2. Read the following verses and record your thoughts about the light they shed on interacting with your clan. The list is long, but don't hurry through it. Split these questions over two or three days if necessary in order to let the full weight of each passage sink into your heart and solidify in your mind.

    ♥ Ephesians 4:2–3

    _____

    _____

    ♥ Luke 6:31

    _____

    _____

    ♥ Romans 12:9

    _____

    _____

    ♥ 1 Peter 4:8

    _____

    _____

    ♥ 1 John 4:7

    _____

    _____

♥ 1 John 4:18–19

_____

_____

♥ Proverbs 10:12

_____

_____

♥ Luke 6:35

_____

_____

♥ Matthew 22:37–39

_____

_____

♥ 1 Peter 3:7–9

_____

_____

♥ Exodus 20:12

_____

_____

♥ 1 John 4:8 (OUCH!!!!)

_____

_____

Now, how would you summarize in your own words what the Bible teaches about treating others—especially our family members? It doesn't have to be an exhaustive paragraph, just a few simple sentences that highlight the principles that most stuck in your mind as you pondered them.

_____

_____

_____

My kids are right. With others I am polite. Always the people pleaser, I want to be liked. I don't want to lose friends. I don't want to offend someone and risk the chance that they might not like me. And so outside our home I verbally hold it together. But often with my own family I let down my guard and let harsh words fly. I don't control my temper and I don't temper my words. Shame on me. But I suspect I'm not alone.

LISTEN, LOVE, REPEAT, PAGES 193–194

3. Sometimes we are tempted to use harsh language or display an agitated demeanor when answering a relative's question—especially one from our spouse or child. Read Proverbs 15:1. Have you ever been guilty of not giving a gentle or soft answer when being asked a question by a family member? Yep, we all have!

   In retrospect—and based on what you have learned in this week's study—how can you soften your answers to your family members so your words don't escalate a conversation, stirring up wrath?

   _____

   _____

   _____

   _____

4. What is the most important lesson about interacting with your family members from this study that you want to allow to alter your thinking or your behavior? How would you say it in a sentence? Once you have your sentence, program a reminder on your phone or email to send to yourself a week or two from now. When it arrives, evaluate yourself to see if you have made any progress in this area.

   _____

   _____

   _____

   _____

5. CHALLENGE IDEAS: This session's challenge is to detonate a love bomb for one of your family members, showing your affection for them and your gratefulness to God that they are part of your family. First, spend a few moments praying about who might be the target of your love bomb. Then, write that person's name here:

I choose _____ as the target of my love bomb.

Next, choose one of the ideas below, or make up one of your own. It can be something sweet and simple, or a more involved idea. Then, shower your family member with adoration and acceptance as you launch the love bomb in their direction. Don't forget to pencil this in on your schedule right now so you don't forget!

♥ Use lipstick or a wax pencil to write a message of love to a family member on the bathroom mirror or windshield of their car.

♥ Leave your child's favorite treat on their pillow during the day so they will discover it when they get ready for bed. Attach a note to it telling them one thing you love about them.

♥ When packing your child's lunch for school, write a message of love on a banana with a ballpoint pen. Sign it "From your fruity mom."

♥ Purchase tickets to a musical or sporting event that you know your spouse or other family member (not you, necessarily!) would love to go to. Tuck the tickets in a card and mail it to their place of employment so they will receive it during the workday. Then, go with them to the event, even though it isn't really your thing.

♥ While your spouse or other family member is at work, decorate their car with balloons and streamers. Place a sign on it that reads: "This car belongs to an amazing husband!" (Or son or daughter or aunt or uncle. You get the picture!)

♥ Go without buying yourself any fancy coffee or snacks for a month or two. Save up the money you would have spent on those items and instead give it to one of your children, slipped inside a card. On the card, write a note telling them how much you love them and that you are treating them to a shopping spree with the enclosed money.

♥ Cook your spouse's favorite meal one night this week, including a main dish, side dish, and dessert. Send them a text message beforehand asking them to name these favorite foods and to also choose a night that they would like to have their special supper. When they ask why you are doing it, simply tell them, "Just because I'm glad I married you."

♥ Take one of your children to see a movie with you alone—no other siblings allowed. Permit them to select the show. Let them buy popcorn and a soft drink, even if you never normally grant permission for them to purchase munchies.

♥ Pack a picnic lunch and take one of your children to a park. Play with them on the playground equipment or fly a kite together. Spend some unrushed time, just the two of you.

♥ Snoop around a little bit by asking your spouse's parent what their favorite book, toy, or board game was when they were young. Then, log onto an online auction site such as eBay to see if you can find it to purchase for them. You can also do this for an extended family member.

♥ Arrange for your spouse (or other relative) to have a Saturday out with a few of their friends. Make up a coupon on your computer—or hand write one on paper—telling them that they will be treated to a day away with their friends, doing whatever it is that they enjoy. Tell them you will happily hold down the fort while they are gone.

Scripture Memory Verse of the Week Reminder

Wow, think of all the Scripture you've been memorizing over the course of this study! Practice aloud the verse for this session one more time (see page 106).

The Boomerang of Blessing

For we are God's handiwork, created in Christ Jesus to do good works, which God prepared in advance for us to do.

(EPHESIANS 2:10)

———————— Checking In (10 minutes) ————————

Welcome to the final session of *Listen, Love, Repeat*. Can you believe this is our last time together? An important part of this study is sharing what you have learned from reading the book and from completing your between-sessions personal study. Remember, you are still welcome at the study even if you weren't able to complete the material.

♥ What from the session five video segment most challenged or encouraged you since the group last met?

_____

_____

_____

_____

♥ What insights did you discover from your reading of chapter 9 of the *Listen, Love, Repeat* book?

_____

_____

_____

_____

♥ What did you get out of the between-sessions personal study?

_____

_____

_____

_____

♥ What did you do for last session's challenge—detonating a love bomb for someone in your family? What were the results? Or, if you haven't done it yet, what gesture are you planning?

_____

_____

_____

_____

─────── Video: The Boomerang of Blessing (28 minutes) ───────

Play the video segment for session six. As you watch, record any thoughts or concepts that stand out to you in the outline that follows.

NOTES

Wouldn't it be mind-blowing to trace your ancestry of faith all the way back to the early church and see if there might be a person mentioned in the Bible who is in your spiritual family tree?

_____

_____

_____

In Acts 9:36–42 we encounter a one-sentence description of a little-known Bible character. Verse 36 says, "In Joppa there was a disciple named Tabitha (in Greek her name is Dorcas); *she was always doing good and helping the poor.*"

_____

_____

_____

Good here in the Greek means "good nature that originates from God and is empowered by him through faith" and *always doing* was actually one word in the Greek. It meant "to continually make happen or to manufacture." Tabitha invented ways to do good to others–she manufactured kindness!

_____

_____

_____

What will be your one-sentence eulogy?

_____

_____

It has been said that there are two types of people in the world: those who enter a room full of people and narcissistically announce, "Here I am!" and those who walk into a room, seek out someone, and lovingly declare, "There you are!"

_____

_____

_____

_____

_____

Many religions are based on a good works mentality—if you just do enough good, God will give you a ticket to heaven. Christianity is just the opposite. It says we will never be good enough. Ever. That is why Jesus died for us.

_____

_____

_____

_____

_____

We are not saved by our good works. We are saved in order to do good works.

_____

_____

_____

_____

_____

When we are careful to weigh ALL that the Bible says about good works—especially Ephesians 2:8–10 and James 2:14–17—we can think about them this way: We are saved by grace—not by works. BUT God prepared works in advance for us to do. Works by themselves don't get us to heaven. However, just *saying* you have faith—by itself—without any accompanying works is a dead faith.

_____

_____

_____

_____

BOTTOM LINE: Good works are not our ticket to heaven. They are our marching orders here on earth.

_____

_____

_____

_____

Our kindness can help others to discover God's grace and accept his salvation (Romans 2:4).

_____

_____

_____

_____

Kindness in Romans 2:4 is an adjective that is really a combination of two words—*kind* and *useful*. We don't have any equivalent English word. It actually means both thoughtful *and* eternally useful. It serves a purpose—it leads others to repentance.

_____

_____

_____

_____

When we reflect God's kindness, it can lead others to repentance.

_____

_____

_____

_____

A boomerang is an interesting contraption. It is a device made from two blades—called arms—connected at the proper angle, each arm serving as an airfoil. An airfoil is a curved structure designed to do one thing—to lift.

_____

_____

_____

_____

If we use our two outstretched arms to lift others up, sometimes the boomerang of blessing lands right back in our life.

_____

_____

_____

_____

——————————— Group Discussion (10 minutes) ———————————

Take a few minutes to discuss what you just watched.

1. What part of the teaching had the most impact on you?

   _____

   _____

   _____

   _____

2. What are your thoughts about tracing your spiritual family tree? Who was it that told you about following Christ in such a way that you wanted to become a believer? Do you know who led *that person* to the Lord?

   _____

   _____

   _____

   _____

3. Why do you think the concept of scattering kindness is so needed in our culture today? What seems to be scattered throughout our world instead—the things we hear about daily in the news or on our social media feeds?

   _____

   _____

   _____

   _____

4. Karen talked in the video about two types of people in the world: those who enter a room and announce, "Here I am!" and those who walk into a room,

seek out someone else, and lovingly declare, "There you are!" The world is full of the first type of person. However, the biblical character Tabitha must have been the second type of person. Have you ever known someone of either type? Share about their behavior–but please do not use their name if they are the first type of person!

_____

_____

_____

_____

———— Cluster Group Discussion (8 minutes) ————

If your group is comprised of more than twelve members, consider completing this discussion in smaller groups of three to six people each.

5. In the video teaching, Karen talked about good works. Many religions have a mentality that promises that if you do enough good works, it will cancel out any of your bad behavior, thereby earning you a ticket to heaven. Take turns having members read aloud the passages below, noting what they teach about good works and faith. Then, answer the questions that follow.

♥ 2 Timothy 1:9–10

_____

_____

♥ Romans 11:5–6

_____

_____

♥ Ephesians 2:8–10

_____

_____

♥ Romans 3:27–28

_____

_____

♥ James 2:14–17

_____

_____

How would you explain to someone the role of good works in the life of the Christian?

_____

_____

_____

_____

Karen explained the role of good works by saying: "Good works are not our ticket to heaven. They are our marching orders here on earth." What is another phrase your group can come up with along these lines? Fill in the blanks: Good works are not _____. However, they are _____.

———————— Group Discussion (12 minutes) ————————

Gather back together as one large group and answer the following questions.

6. Have individual groups share the fill-in-the-blank sentence they came up with that summarizes the Bible's teaching on good works.

_____

_____

_____

_____

7. Have someone read Paul's words in Romans 2:1–4 to the group, and then discuss the following questions:

♥ Why do you think it is easy to judge others without recognizing that we ourselves are not perfect? In fact, we even sometimes do the same things!

_____

_____

_____

_____

♥ What does verse 4 claim is the reason for God's kindness? What other characteristics of God besides kindness are also listed in this verse? You may want to read the verse in various translations to get a clearer picture. Or, do an Internet search of the definition of each word in order to fully understand the subtle difference in meanings between them.

_____

_____

_____

_____

♥ Which of these characteristics is hardest for you to display and why?

_____

_____

_____

_____

8. Have someone read Titus 3:1–8 aloud to the group as the rest of you follow along. Then answer the questions below:

♥ What seven things do verses 1–2 encourage Christians to do?

_____

_____

_____

_____

♥ One concept is mentioned twice in this passage. What do both verses 1 and 8 say believers are supposed to do?

_____

_____

_____

_____

♥ Verse 8 doesn't just mention that it is a nifty idea to do good to others. It urges us to "be careful to devote" ourselves to doing good. On a scale of 1 to 10, with 1 being "careless and apathetic" and 10 being "extremely careful and fully devoted," what number would you rate yourself when it comes to making doing good your aim in daily life? How can applying what you have learned throughout this study help that number to improve?

_____

_____

_____

_____

♥ Look at the end of verse 8. What word is used to describe the good things believers do? For whom does it say doing good is beneficial?

_____

_____

_____

_____

♥ Look one more time at the passage, carefully noticing the "before" language used in describing Christians. Then, think about your own story when it comes to what you were like before you became a follower of Jesus. For those who wish to share, speak the following sentence, filling in the blank with words that describe your own experience: *At one time I was _____, but when the kindness and love of our Savior appeared, he saved me—not because of the righteous things I had done, but because of his great mercy.*

9. Turn to 2 Corinthians 6:1–13. Have one group member read the passage aloud as everyone else follows along. Then answer the questions below:

♥ Look back over the passage and list any situations, circumstances, or other issues affecting Paul and his companions that were negative at best or even seriously dangerous. Go slowly. There are many!

_____

_____

_____

_____

♥ Go through the passage again, this time looking for the way Paul and his companions responded—not with anger or retaliation—but in ways that honored God and reflected his character. Again, take your time. There are many!

_____

_____

_____

_____

♥ How does combing through this passage and seeing the difficulties Paul and his fellow believers were up against—along with the way they responded—challenge, inspire, puzzle, or convict you? When you are treated in a bad manner that is far less serious, do you respond likewise?

_____

_____

_____

_____

> The generous will prosper; those who refresh others will themselves be refreshed.
>
> (PROVERBS 11:25 NLT)

10. BONUS QUESTION: Recall that in the video teaching Karen mentioned that *God's kindness* in the Greek is defined as being both thoughtful and eternally useful. Does anyone have a story of how the heartfelt kindness of a Christian was not only thoughtful but useful in leading someone to pursue a relationship with the Lord? Share it with the group.

_____

_____

_____

_____

11. BONUS QUESTION: Briefly review the notes you took in this study guide over the course of the group's time together during the six sessions and be ready to share one insight that really grabbed your attention. Was there a story told that really inspired you? A single verse or larger chunk of Scripture that spoke to your soul and motivated, changed, or convicted you? Spend a few moments allowing those who wish to share their takeaway to do so.

_____

_____

_____

_____

———— Session 6 Memory Verse (1 minute) ————

As a group, read aloud this final session's memory verse:

> For we are God's handiwork, created in Christ Jesus to do good works, which God prepared in advance for us to do.
>
> (EPHESIANS 2:10)

——— Challenge Reminder and Closing Prayer (2 minutes) ———

CHALLENGE: The challenge this session is to scatter kindness in secret! This week, choose a person to whom you can show love, help financially, or toss a little kindness their way. However, do it completely anonymously, so that nobody else will know—only God.

PRAYER: Have one person close in prayer, thanking God for the work he has done and the growth he has caused in each of your lives in learning to live alert, scatter kindness, and be a tool in reaching the lost for him.

Discussion: Seventh Bonus Session?

Discuss whether or not you're going to meet for a seventh bonus session. (If you decide to move forward, your facilitator will need to be sure to read the session seven content thoroughly to bring any needed materials to class!) There will be no teaching video in this session, but you will have ample time to share what you've learned in your final personal study, and there will be reflection questions to discuss as a group. The session outline also includes a few hands-on group reflection activities. And of course there will be food and fun—a sort of wrap-up *Listen, Love, Repeat* party! Several recipe suggestions are provided in the bonus material section in the back of this study guide. These treats are also perfect for sharing with others in your life as you scatter kindness.

Take a minute now to look over the three food-theme ideas (a cookie bar, a mug & muffin night, or a fruit fest) and decide which one—if any—your group will do. Both involve the group splitting off two-by-two to scatter a little kindness to people you know or even strangers, then to reconvene to share the results.

Remember to use the hash tag #listenloverepeat when posting any of your ideas or feedback on social media. We don't do this to say, "Look at me!" We do it in order to say, "Well, will you look at Jesus!" (Check out the three food-themed ideas now [pages 136–137] and decide if you will do them.)

Final Personal Study

SESSION 6

We are useful to the Master, even though we may appear to be common. He has good works planned in advance for us to do. We just need to have an open heart, and a listening ear, as we seek to be available to do good to others.

Years from now, how do you want people to remember you? Take a little time today to think about what actions of yours speak the loudest. What will be your one-sentence eulogy?

LISTEN, LOVE, REPEAT, PAGE 214

Special Note

We have come to the last section of personal study. If your group has decided to meet for a seventh bonus session, you will be able to share your thoughts on this section when you get together. If your group has chosen not to meet once more, this section is for your reflection only and is designed to help drive home the main message of *Listen, Love, Repeat*. Happy studying!

Challenge Reminder

The challenge this session is to scatter kindness in secret! This week, choose a person to whom you can show love, help financially, or toss a little kindness their way. However, do it completely anonymously, so that nobody else will know—only God.

You might sneak an envelope of cash with an encouraging note in the purse of a financially struggling single mom at work. Or, have flowers or chocolate-covered strawberries delivered to someone anonymously with a note telling them you are praying for them. Or, anonymously pay for a young family's dinner when you see them eating out and trying their best to be patient with their restless kids. Or, stealthily leave a bag of canned goods on the back porch of a family whose main breadwinner has just been laid off. Or, send a coffee house, salon, spa, or department store gift card to a friend whose husband has just left her; tell her it is a gift from God and he just wants her to know how beautiful he thinks she is.

So decide on your special someone and plan your secret act of kindness now. Then be sure to write it on your schedule or program a reminder on your phone so that you don't forget!

Session 6 Memory Verse

Below is the memory verse for this session. Write it on a notecard, type it in the notes app on your phone, or photocopy and cut out the version found on page 158. Set an alarm for at least two times a day when you know you will have a minute to look over the verse and commit it to memory.

> For we are God's handiwork, created in Christ Jesus to do good works, which God prepared in advance for us to do.
>
> (EPHESIANS 2:10)

Read and Learn

Read chapter 10 of the *Listen, Love, Repeat* book and record any thoughts or insights you discovered in the space provided.

_____

_____

_____

_____

_____

Study and Reflect

1. Think back to your life before you started this study. On a scale of 1 to 10 (with 1 being "never" and 10 being "always"), what number would you have rated yourself when it comes to how often you lived alert—being on the lookout for ways to scatter kindness and show someone God's love?

_____

_____

What number would you rate yourself now? Has the number changed? Or, do you have a desire to see that number change? Explain.

_____

_____

_____

_____

> No, we are not saved by our good works. But we are saved in order *to do* good works. Ephesians 2:10 even goes so far as to assert that God planned since creation for us to do kind deeds: "For we are God's handiwork, created in Christ Jesus to do good works, which God prepared in advance for us to do." We can think about it this way: good works aren't our ticket to heaven. They are our marching orders here on Earth.
>
> LISTEN, LOVE, REPEAT, PAGE 216

2. Of all the stories, examples, Scripture passages, and group conversations during the course of the *Listen, Love, Repeat* study, which one has clung to your heart and mind or challenged you the most? Why?

_____

_____

_____

_____

3. Take the next few days to think about the many areas we've covered (listed on pages 130–131) as we have studied about living alert, scattering kindness, and reflecting God's love. Spend a few minutes during these few days praying over the list. Circle any of the areas where you feel God calling you to pay more careful attention, listening for heart drops and then following them up with an act of love.

♥ Friends

_____

_____

_____

♥ Coworkers

_____

_____

_____

♥ Neighbors

_____

_____

_____

♥ Necessary people

_____

_____

_____

♥ Church, community, or other acquaintances

_____

_____

_____

♥ The grieving

_____

_____

_____

♥ The lonely

_____

_____

_____

♥ The marginalized and less-than-lovely in society

_____

_____

_____

♥ The hard-to-love

_____

_____

_____

♥ Guests (or potential guests, if you are hospitably hesitant!)

_____

_____

_____

♥ Immediate family

_____

_____

_____

♥ Extended family

_____

_____

_____

♥ Strangers

_____

_____

_____

Now, look back at the categories you circled and do two things. First, after the circled category, write the name of the person or persons from that category you feel called to focus on. Then, after their name, jot down one action you could take in order to listen to them more closely or show love to them in a tangible way.

Scripture Memory Verse of the Week Reminder

Briefly review not just this session's memory verse (see page 128) but the other five as well (pages 157–158). Choose one that you want to make your goal to live out. If you have not already done so, post it in a prominent place where you will see it often. Read it. Ponder it. Memorize it. Live it.

Prayer of Commitment

Close this study in prayer. Ask God to continue to guide you as you seek to learn to live alert, listening for heart drops and loving others, pointing them toward Christ. Make this prayer time one of commitment to living a life that reflects God's thoughtful and eternally useful kindness that can lead others to spend eternity with him.

Final Note from the Author

Wouldn't it be wonderful if we were sitting across from each other, enjoying a steaming cup of coconut mocha (my favorite!) or an icy glass of herbal mint tea? I would love to hear how this study has impacted you. I pray that hearing my stories and studying the various Bible passages in this guide has motivated you to live alert, listening for heart drops and scattering kindness.

Our world today is full of heartache and turmoil. People are scared. Families are fractured. Individuals are lonely and in need of some human compassion. In person and online we witness criticism, combativeness, and sometimes outright hate. But we do not need to follow suit. We can choose to behave differently.

Let's together, you and I, start a movement–a movement to listen and love, touching other human beings with the love of Christ. It won't be based on a lofty notion or complicated theological concept. We just need to learn to do what Jesus did–to notice the one who least expects to be seen. To listen between the lines as we hear others speak. To ask the Holy Spirit to tap on our hearts, enable us to create wiggle room in our schedules, and then empower us to look beyond ourselves to what act of kindness we might perform that will cheer up another human soul.

It may be someone who lives in your home. It might be an extended family member. Perhaps it will be a "necessary person." Or even someone in your life who is difficult to love (gulp!). It could be a complete stranger. Just know that today, somewhere and somehow, you will cross paths with a person who needs to know someone cares. Remember, ministry for Jesus was often the person standing right in front of him. Who is that for you today?

I cannot wait to see the fruit that comes from your willingness to open your heart to all God is teaching you about sharing his love with others. Be sure to use the hashtag #listenloverepeat when posting on social media about what you have learned—not to draw attention to yourself, but to point others to God. May your actions and your words bless many on his behalf as you seek to make him famous.

Now it is time for me to use my words one last time—this time as I have the privilege of praying for you.

Father, thank you for the kindness you have shown us. And thank you for the immeasurable grace and mercy you demonstrated toward us by sending your Son Jesus to die on the cross, taking our sins upon himself and providing a way for us to spend eternity with you in heaven.

I pray for the person who now holds this book in her hands. Bless her. Encourage her. Grant her creative ideas for reaching out to others. Enable her to carve out time in her schedule to listen and to love. May her ears be ever tuned to your voice. May she become skilled at listening between the lines, hearing the heart drops of others. May she reflect your kindness to the people in her corner of the world as she loves and serves you by loving and serving others—in your strength and through your power.

Help her conversations and conduct to be conduits for your love. May her very life be poured out lavishly as she interacts with a lost and hurting world. And, most of all, may you receive every drop of glory for the good works that are done—the works you have prepared in advance for your children to do while here on earth.

What an immense privilege and humbling honor it is to serve you by loving and serving others—all of whom are made in your image. In Jesus' name, amen.

Leader Instructions

Now that the six regular sessions have come to a close, your group might like to meet for one more bonus session as a wrap-up—even a party! This is strongly recommended because it helps to tie together and drive home the main point of the whole study. During your time together you will discuss the session six personal study, including the final chapter of *Listen, Love, Repeat.* You may also choose to commemorate these past weeks with a little party, using the yummy recipes included in this guide to help you celebrate!

In addition to discussion questions, session seven includes a few hands-on reflection activities for your group to engage in. There also are a few take-home reminder gift ideas to help them live a life of welcome. Feel free to set the length of your bonus session. It can be anywhere from an hour to an entire slumber party!

If you add a bonus session seven, thoroughly read the session beforehand to coordinate the menu and food preparation—should you care to offer refreshments—and to purchase items for the activities you decide to include. You may wish to ask members for a suggested donation of a few dollars each to cover the cost of the materials for any activities, beverages, or the take-home reminders. Or, if you are doing the study through a church, you may have money in the budget for these expenses.

———————————— Step One: Food ————————————

Options for refreshments can be as simple or involved as you'd like. First, you may simply ask everyone to bring a dish to pass. These can be dishes that round out an entire meal or just simple fingers foods and appetizers. It might be a dip night where everyone brings a different dip to pass along with some crackers or chips.

Or—if you want to take it up a notch and include a classic *Listen, Love, Repeat* activity—you can select one of the following three ideas:

COOKIE BAR

Host a cookie bar with every member bringing two dozen of their favorite drop cookie or bar cookie recipe. Also bring disposable plates, plastic wrap, ribbon, and scissors. Additionally, run off several copies of the ready-made "You've Been Love Bombed" tags found on page 155. Then, after the session, package up several plates of the remaining cookies, adding a ribbon and tag to each one. Venture out in pairs to take them to people in your church and community, showering them with love. If you wish, you may ask recipients if they have any prayer requests. And then—pray with them right there! You will be scattering kindness by love bombing your community.

MUG & MUFFIN NIGHT

This is the same basic concept as the cookie bar, but with a twist. Ask members to bring a dozen muffins each and to also bring a mug from home. You will provide coffee, tea, and/or hot cocoa. They will enjoy it in their mug. They'll also munch on a muffin or two. Then, you will package up the remaining marvelous muffins and go out in pairs to deliver them, setting off several love bombs!

FRUIT FEST

This is a fruity version of the above ideas but equally delicious. Instead of serving cookies or muffins, have everyone bring their favorite fruit-based dish. It might be apples and a yummy cream cheese dip, a crisp or cobbler, a tropical fruit salad, a carved watermelon bowl full of fresh fruit, a dried fruit-and-nut trail mix, or chunks of fruit with a chocolate fountain. Also have members bring various fresh fruits—at least six to eight pieces each. These fruits can be gift-wrapped on the plates (or you could purchase small baskets from dollar or second-hand stores) and delivered during the meeting.

LOVE BOMB YOUR COMMUNITY

Deliver your treats or fruit baskets to any of the folks below or come up with your own ideas: (NOTE: You may need to call ahead to ask permission from some of the suggested places.)

- ♥ Church staff
- ♥ Grocery or department store workers
- ♥ Police officers, fire fighters, ambulance drivers
- ♥ People pumping gas at a neighborhood station
- ♥ Shut-ins from your church
- ♥ Residents from a local retirement community or nursing home
- ♥ Local school employees
- ♥ People driving away from a fast food drive-thru
- ♥ Custodians at the shopping mall
- ♥ Baristas at the coffee houses around town
- ♥ Bell-ringers at the department stores during the holidays
- ♥ Groups of teens wandering at the local mall or hanging out in an arcade
- ♥ Children's workers and Sunday school teachers from your church
- ♥ City council or school board members
- ♥ Bank tellers, salon stylists, gas station attendants, workers at convenience stores
- ♥ Your local television or radio station employees
- ♥ _____ (you fill in the blank!)

——————— Step Two: Memento Reminder Gift ———————

As a memento and a reminder to continue to scatter kindness to others, you might choose to give every group member one of the following items as a final session gift. Whenever she sees or uses it, she will be reminded of what she learned during the study time together.

♥ A journal and pen for recording ideas for reaching out

♥ Stationery or note cards for penning letters of love to others

♥ A coffee house gift card with instructions to listen that week for who could use a pick-me-up. Then invite that person out for coffee.

♥ A bracelet or necklace with a heart on it to remind them to love

♥ A candle to burn while they spend time with God each day

♥ A small bottle of perfume or scented lotion. Make and attach a handwritten or scrapbooking-type tag or use the ready-made one on page 155 that includes the following verse: *"But thanks be to God, who always leads us as captives in Christ's triumphal procession and uses us to spread the aroma of the knowledge of him everywhere." (2 Corinthians 2:14)*

♥ A packet of flower seeds to plant. When the flowers are full grown, instruct them to cut the flowers and give them as a cheery gift.

♥ A potted Shasta daisy or black-eyed Susan plant. When the flowers are in full bloom, they can cut and give them to a neighbor or necessary person.

♥ Wind chimes. When they hear them ring, they will be reminded to listen closely between the lines during conversations to hear a heart drop.

Step Three: Materials and Supplies

Make sure to read through the bonus session beforehand to familiarize yourself with any materials and supplies you might need. These include the memento reminder gifts and possible gift tags (found on page 155) for the attendees, photocopies of the *Top Ten Most Wanted List* for the members (found on page 146). Also, don't forget disposable plates, plastic wrap, ribbon, and scissors for taking treats out into the community along with enough copies of the ready-made "You've Been Love Bombed" tags found on page 155 to tie onto the plates of goodies. If you are doing the fruit fest idea, you may want to purchase small baskets to use instead of plates.

Other-Centered Living in a Self-Centered World

Opener

For fun, have everyone answer the following question:

If someone were to treat you to a little something from the list below (see page 140), which would you choose and what specifically would it be?

Have everyone listen closely to each other's answers. Then, later on down the line, if God nudges you to do something special for one of your fellow group members, you will have an idea of their likes.

♥ A drink from a coffee house

♥ My favorite restaurant take-out item

♥ A book I have been eager to read

♥ A basket of my four favorite fruits

♥ Tickets to a movie I would like to see

♥ My favorite candy bar

♥ A new fun bottle of nail polish (tell what color)

Group Discussion

1. Since the group was last together, we read chapter ten of *Listen, Love, Repeat*. Take a few moments to glance back over that chapter. Was there anything you highlighted, were struck by, or had a question about in your reading? Share your thoughts with the group.

_____

_____

_____

_____

2. In chapter ten of *Listen, Love, Repeat*, Karen discusses three types of judgment mentioned in Scripture. Two are permissible, but one we should never do. Here is a short recap:

♥ *Diakrino* is best explained as "to discriminate or arbitrate between two people or things."

♥ *Anakrino* is translated "to examine, question, investigate, and discern."

♥ *Krino* means "to form an opinion of and then to pronounce a sentence or condemn."

In short, it is fine for us to have processes in place that will arbitrate disputes. It is fine for us to evaluate, question, investigate, and discern so we can make informed decisions. But it is *never* okay for us to condemn someone else. Does this explanation of judging help you better to understand what the Bible teaches on this topic? If so, how?

_____

_____

_____

Here are some examples. It is *not* okay for us to look at someone's lifestyle choices and behavior and pronounce a sentence on them—labeling them with a derogatory name. That would be *krino*.

It *is* okay to discern if someone is a good influence on us due to their behavior, and if not, to limit the time we spend with them so as not to be tempted to do wrong ourselves. This would be an example of *anakrino*.

And it is all right for us to decide, when the cookie jar is empty, which of our two children ate the last one—even though both of them deny it—since moms can usually tell when a child is not telling the truth! This would be an example of *diakrino*.

What other examples can you come up with?

_____

_____

_____

_____

Individual Activity: What Is God Asking Me to Do?

On your own, ask God to bring to mind someone who you once judged. Perhaps you labeled them as a bad person, even if only in your thoughts. Or, maybe you spoke ill of them to someone else. Perhaps you were behaving in a legalistic way and you questioned their Christianity. Or it might be that you just never were intentional to get to know them because you had already formed a negative opinion of them. Write that person's name below.

_____

Now take a moment to read this passage:

> [10] You, then, why do you judge your brother or sister? Or why do you treat them with contempt? For we will all stand before God's judgment seat. [11] It is written: "As surely as I live," says the Lord, "every knee will bow before me; every tongue will acknowledge God." [12] So then, each of us will give an account of ourselves to God. [13] Therefore let us stop passing judgment on one another. Instead, make up your mind not to put any stumbling block or obstacle in the way of a brother or sister.
>
> (ROMANS 14:10–13)

What do you notice about this passage? What word is used for how we treat others when we judge? Write it below and also write in which verse you found the word. Then, look up the meaning of this word online on your phone and write out the definition.

Word: _____

Verse: _____

Meaning: _____

Who exactly does this passage say is supposed to be doing the judging? What will we have to do when that judgment takes place? Also list which verse tells what we will one day have to do.

Who will judge: _____

What we will have to do: _____

Verse: _____

Did you catch this important distinction? We are not to pass judgment on others, treating them with contempt (verse 10). God alone is the great and final judge and we will one day have to answer to him, giving an account for how we behaved (verse 12). So, let's remember this phrase:

I will refrain from verse 10 livin', or I will have some
verse 12 answer-givin' to do on judgment day!

Copy this phrase in the space below in your own handwriting. If this is an area where you really struggle, when you get home, write it on a notecard and place it where you will be reminded of this saying often.

_____

_____

_____

Finally, ask the Lord to persistently nudge you if he wants you to ask for forgiveness in person (or by letter, phone call, or email) from someone you have treated with contempt or wrongly judged, even if it was a long time ago. Please realize this is not always necessary, and it may open old wounds or previous relationship tensions, especially if the other person never realized how you felt about them. Be careful and prayerful as you decide what to do. You may wish instead to write a prayer to God about this person and then resolve to treat them differently in the future.

Group Discussion

Gather as one large group again for the following questions:

3. The first question in the session six personal study was this: *Think back to your life before you started this study. On a scale of 1 to 10 (with 1 being "never" and 10 being "always"), what number would you have rated yourself when it comes to how often you lived alert—being on the lookout for ways to scatter kindness and show someone God's love? Has that number changed at all? Or, do you have a desire to see that number improve? Explain.*

   Share the answers you wrote, if you are willing. And then share your goals for how you want to live in the future when it comes to listening and loving, becoming someone who does acts of kindness for friends and foes alike.

   _____

   _____

   _____

   _____

4. As you look back over the book and study guide, what verses of Scripture have been most meaningful to you, and why?

_____

_____

_____

_____

5. Of the Bible characters and stories covered in the book and study, did one particularly stand out to you? Why? They are listed here for you to review:

♥ Jesus, Jairus, and the unnamed ill woman who touched Jesus—chapter one

♥ The Thessalonian church and Paul, who "shared his very life" with them—chapter three

♥ Ruth and her commitment to her mother-in-love Naomi—chapter five

♥ King David and the people who willingly contributed to the building of the temple—chapter six

♥ Jesus in the form of the hungry, thirsty, naked, and imprisoned—chapter seven

♥ Tabitha, the woman who manufactured kindness—chapter ten

_____

_____

_____

_____

6. If you could pick just one concept, idea, story, warning, or encouragement from *Listen, Love, Repeat*, which would you most likely be able to recall a year from now? Why do you think it impacted you so deeply?

_____

_____

_____

_____

Individual Activity: My Top Ten Most Wanted List

(**Leaders:** Distribute copies of the *Top Ten Most Wanted List*. See the next page.)

Think for a moment about all of the people you encounter throughout the year—family, extended family, friends, coworkers, neighbors, necessary people, acquaintances, church members, the lonely, the marginalized, the hard-to-love, and even complete strangers. Next, craft a "Top Ten Most Wanted" list: people to whom you want to show love over the course of the next year. You may know their actual names, or just their titles or descriptions—the mail carrier, the barista at the coffeehouse, etc. You will choose one person per month—and because there are twelve months but only ten people, it will give you a little wiggle room if you miss a month.

You can write the names on the next page for now, but then use the designed copy you just received from your leader for your final list. Post it where you will see it often, or slip it into your Bible. Be sure to check off each name as you shower that person with an act of kindness.

Final Prayer

Have one member close the group in prayer; also pray a thankful blessing over the food you are about to enjoy (and your group venture to deliver the extra cookies, muffins, or fruit). Or, if you wish, you may have the women break into groups of two to four for closing prayer.

Top Ten Most Wanted List

Here are the ten people I most desire to touch with an act of kindness over the course of the next year:

1. _____
2. _____
3. _____
4. _____
5. _____
6. _____
7. _____
8. _____
9. _____
10. _____

♥ ♥ ♥

Therefore, as we have opportunity, let us do good to all people, especially to those who belong to the family of believers.

(GALATIANS 6:10)

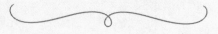

Let's Eat and Then Go Scatter Kindness!

Now is the time to enjoy your refreshments. When you are done eating, use the leftover food items to package up plates of goodies to take out into the community on your love bombing mission. Set a time to return, and when members come back, spend a little time sharing about the experience.

To help you get cooking, the following are some of Karen's favorite muffin and cookie recipes along with a yummy fruit dip. Make them for your bonus session or any time you want to share with others as you scatter kindness.

COOKIES

Lemon-Drop Delights

The perfect blend of tart and sweet. Reminds me of a lazy summer day.

INGREDIENTS:

½ c. butter, softened

¾ c. sugar

1 egg

1 T. half-and-half creamer

2 t. finely grated lemon peel

¼ t. vanilla extract

1½ c. all-purpose flour

½ c. finely crushed lemon drops

1 t. baking powder

¼ t. salt

In a large bowl, cream the butter and sugar with a hand mixer on medium speed until it is light and fluffy. Mix in egg, half-and-half, lemon peel, and vanilla extract. In a separate bowl combine the remaining dry ingredients. Gradually mix the dry ingredients into the butter mixture, being careful not to overmix. Cover and chill dough for one hour. Drop batter by heaping teaspoons about 3 inches apart onto well-greased cookie sheets. Bake at 350 degrees for 8–10 minutes, being careful not to overbake. Allow cookies to cool for 5 minutes before transferring to a wire cooling rack. Makes about 3 dozen cookies. ♥

Grandma Gig's Oatmeal Walnut Cookies

Karen's stepmom's famous recipe. They won a blue ribbon at the Grand Traverse (Mich.) county fair in the 1950s. When shopping for ingredients, don't forget powdered sugar to roll them in before baking.

CREAM TOGETHER IN A LARGE BOWL USING A HAND MIXER ON MEDIUM SPEED:

2 c. brown sugar

2 sticks real butter, softened

MIX IN:

2 eggs

1 t. vanilla extract

IN ANOTHER BOWL MIX:

2 c. all-purpose flour

1 t. salt

1 t. baking soda

3 c. quick-cook oats

1 c. chopped walnuts

Combine wet and dry ingredients, being careful not to overmix. Chill dough, covered, for 4 hours or overnight. Roll into 1½-inch balls. Roll in powdered sugar. Place on ungreased cookie sheet and bake 10–13 minutes at 350 degrees or until lightly golden. Do not overbake. Makes about 5 dozen cookies. ♥

Peanut Crunch No-Bake Cookies

These will remind you of a Payday candy bar. Karen's husband and boys just can't get enough of these. Super simple and yet scrumptious.

INGREDIENTS:

1 c. corn syrup

1 c. white sugar

1 c. creamy peanut butter

1 t. vanilla

6 c. Rice Chex brand cereal

1 c. dry roasted and lightly salted peanuts

Optional: 1 c. semi-sweet chocolate chips

Place Rice Chex and peanuts in a large bowl. In a medium-size sauce pan over medium high heat, bring the corn syrup, sugar, and peanut butter to a boil, stirring constantly. Boil for exactly 1 minute. Remove from heat and quickly stir in vanilla. Pour the mixture over the Rice Chex and peanuts and stir gently but quickly. Drop by heaping tablespoons onto wax paper to set up. NOTE: For a really deluxe version, drizzle thin streams of melted semi-sweet chocolate chips over the cookies and allow to harden. Makes 2 to 3 dozen jumbo cookies. ♥

Iced Gingerbread Cookies

Don't just think gingerbread at the holidays. These are great any time of year. Super easy and delightfully delicious!

IN A LARGE SAUCEPAN, BOIL:

1 stick (½ c.) butter

⅔ c. white sugar

1 T. vinegar

½ c. blackstrap molasses

1⅛ t. ground ginger

½ t. cinnamon

⅛ t. allspice

REMOVE FROM HEAT AND ADD:

1/2 t. baking soda that has been dissolved in 2 t. hot water

COOL FOR FIVE MINUTES AND ADD:

1 egg
1 t. baking powder
3 c. all-purpose four

Cover and chill in fridge for 3 hours. Preheat oven to 350 degrees. Roll into 11/2-inch balls. Place on ungreased cookie sheet and bake 10–13 minutes or until lightly golden. Do not overbake. Cool slightly. Then, drizzle icing over.

ICING:

1 c. powdered sugar
1/2 t. vanilla
2–4 T. milk (as needed)

Combine the powdered sugar and vanilla in a small bowl. Thin with a few tablespoons milk until the mixture is of a consistency that can be drizzled over the cookies. Drizzle and let cool completely. ♥

~ MUFFINS ~

Strawberry-Banana Muffins

A moist banana muffin with a surprise strawberry center. Double-yum!

INGREDIENTS:

3/4 c. butter
11/2 c. sugar
1 t. vanilla
1/2 c. buttermilk (not lowfat)
2 eggs, well beaten
11/2 c. mashed ripe bananas
2 c. sifted all-purpose flour
1 t. baking soda
3/4 t. salt
1 c. or more strawberry jam (homemade freezer jam is the bomb!)

In a large bowl, cream butter and sugar until fluffy. Add vanilla. Slowly add in buttermilk and eggs, mixing well. Fold in mashed bananas. In a separate bowl, combine flour, baking soda, and salt. Gently mix the dry ingredients into the wet ingredients, being careful not to overmix. Spray muffin tins with cooking spray or line with muffin cups. Place about a quarter cup of batter in each muffin cup, top with a teaspoon of strawberry jam, and then place a little more batter over the top, making sure it goes all the way to the edges and covers the strawberry jam. Bake at 350 degrees for 18–23 minutes or until a cake tester comes out clean. Do not overbake. Makes 20–24 muffins. ♥

Dried Cherry Oatmeal Muffins with Spiced Crumb Topping

Karen's home state of Michigan is famous for its cherries. Dried tart cherries make this spice-topped treat amazingly tasty!

INGREDIENTS:

1 c. sifted all-purpose flour

1/4 c. sugar

3 t. baking powder

1 c. quick-cooking oats

1/2 t. salt

2/3 c. dried tart cherries

3 T. butter or butter-flavored shortening, melted and slightly cooled

1 egg, beaten

1 c. milk

TOPPING:

2 T. sugar

2 t. all-purpose flour

1 1/4 t. cinnamon

1/4 t. nutmeg

2 t. melted butter

In a small bowl, combine the ingredients for the topping, mixing well. Set aside. In a large bowl, stir together the flour, sugar, baking powder, oats, salt, and cherries. Add in melted butter, egg, and milk. Stir only until the dry ingredients are incorporated with the wet. Fill greased muffin cups two-thirds full. Sprinkle with topping.

Bake at 350 degrees for 18–22 minutes or until a cake tester comes out clean. Do not overbake. Remove from the oven and let cool 5 minutes before removing from the pans. Makes 12 muffins. ♥

Tropical Island Muffins

You'll dream about a sandy beach when you bite into one of these fruity favorites.

INGREDIENTS:

2 c. sifted flour

4 t. baking powder

1/2 t. salt

1/4 c. sugar

2 eggs, well beaten

1 c. milk

1/2 t. pure orange extract

1/4 t. coconut extract

4 T. melted butter, slightly cooled

1/2 c. shredded coconut

1/2 c. chopped almonds, lightly toasted

1 1/2 T. grated orange peel (optional but adds flecks of color)

In a large bowl, combine flour, baking powder, salt, and sugar. Slowly mix in the eggs, milk, extracts, and melted butter, being careful not to overmix. Gently fold in the coconut, almonds, and orange peel. Bake in greased muffin tins (filled two thirds to three quarters full) at 425 degrees for 18–23 minutes or until cake tester comes out clean. Do not over-bake. Makes 12 muffins. ♥

Morning Glory Garden Muffins

Veggies meet fruit in this unique and scrumptious muffin. Packed full of sun-ripened flavor. Serve with cinnamon butter. Simply blend ¼ teaspoon of cinnamon into a stick of room temperature butter and chill slightly.

INGREDIENTS:

2 c. all-purpose flour

1¼ c. sugar

1 T. ground cinnamon

⅛ t. nutmeg

⅛ t. allspice

2 t. baking soda

½ t. salt

3 eggs, lightly beaten

1 c. vegetable oil

1 t. vanilla extract

1 t. almond extract

¾ c. shredded carrots

1 c. shredded zucchini

1 c. chopped, peeled tart apples
(Granny Smith, Braeburn, Golden
Delicious, or Spy)

½ c. crushed pineapple, very well drained

1 c. shredded coconut (or ½ c. coconut
and ½ c. finely chopped walnuts)

In a large bowl, combine flour, sugar, spices, baking soda, and salt. In a separate bowl, mix eggs, oil, and extracts. Stir wet ingredients into dry ingredients just until moistened. Batter will be very thick. Fold in the vegetables and fruits, combining gently and being careful not to overmix. Fill greased or paper lined muffin cups two thirds full. Bake at 350 degrees for 18–22 minutes or until a cake tester inserted into a muffin comes out clean. Cool in the pan 10 minutes before transferring to a wire rack. Makes 18 muffins. ♥

⌁ DIP FOR FRUIT ⌁

Fluffy Fruit Dip

Super simple but delicious. Serve with fresh, whole strawberries, spears of fresh pineapple, or kiwi or apple slices.

INGREDIENTS:

16 oz. cream cheese, room temperature
2—15 oz. jars marshmallow creme

Carefully blend ingredients with a hand mixer on low speed. Serve with fruit. ♥

Quips and Quotables

Following are some portions of the *Listen, Love, Repeat* book that you may wish to photocopy and keep nearby to serve as motivation for you to keep on sharing love with others. As with the memory verses, you can cut them out, put them on card stock, and tape them where you'll see them regularly in your home, office, or car. Or type out a few and put them in your smartphone or computer.

Hearing a heart drop is an art we must lovingly cultivate. It can lead to the most wonderful times of encouragement as we make it our habit to listen and to love.

Jesus wasn't about doing big things. He was about doing the right thing. And often for him, the right thing was noticing *one simple soul.*

Jesus' real ministry *was the person he found standing in front of him. Who is that for you today?*

WE DON'T DO GOOD FOR THE SAKE OF LOOKING GOOD; WE DO GOOD IN ORDER TO POINT OTHERS TO *Jesus.*

Rather than trying to do something grand for God, perhaps we need to embrace the obscure instead. To stop trying to be profound or important and instead just be obedient.

How might the Holy Spirit be tapping on your heart today, prompting you to speak truth, do good, and *share life?*

Don't do good works in order to selfishly shout, "Look at me!" Do them in order to humbly implore, "Will you look at him?"

Don't hang up on your relationships; hang in there instead.

Loving others includes not just giving of our time but feeling with our hearts as well.

Relationships require work. Remembering isn't always easy. And sometimes sweat is involved in LISTENING AND LOVING.

If our perspective each day can be "I am in it for you" instead of "What is in it for me?" we will discover the joy of serving Jesus— without expecting anything in return and done only for an audience of One.

We need to remember our *why*: the reason we love and serve and give thoughtful gifts and do good works. It is so that others will see Jesus. They may *look* at us, but we hope they *see* him.

If there is room in your heart, you'll make room in your home.

Whether you share a book or a bicycle, a cot or a cottage, do it with an attitude of OPENHANDEDNESS and OPENHEARTEDNESS, sharing with others what God has given to you.

Living a life of welcome—opening both your heart and your home—means your stuff gets used. And reused. Over and over again. Your items get nicked and scratched. Your carpet and rugs and linens get stained. While this doesn't mean we don't try to make our surroundings pleasant, it does mean we learn to accept some degree of imperfection. Well-used items often mean that we have loved well.

When we have a God-honoring perspective about our possessions and resources, our hearts and homes can become a *wheelhouse for ministry*.

We can lead with our hearts and bless with our homes, making our homes a haven not only for those who dwell there permanently but for whoever God sends our way.

WHEN WE WILLINGLY OPEN OUR HOMES, WE AREN'T JUST BEING NICE. WE ARE BEING OBEDIENT TO GOD'S WORD.

When we share love with the lonely, the *boomerang of blessing* lands right back in our lap.

We might feel our life is boring and our possessions are plain. Yet there are many who would love to share our seemingly mundane lives, simply to feel that they fit in and that their presence is wanted.

Embracing our less-than-perfect families gives us a picture of how God embraces us.

Judgment does not win others over. Kindness does.

Kindness starts simply.
An encouraging word.
A loving gesture.
A tender sentiment sent through the mail.
A thoughtful small token.
The gift of unhurried time.
A rousing pep talk.
Simply vowing to speak and act in a way that is gentle and kind is the starting point.
Aesop was right:
*"No act of kindness, no matter
how small, is ever wasted."*

Remember that your job is to be kind and willing to share the gospel with others. What happens as a result from your words and actions is up to God. Our job is obedience. *God's job is results.*

SLOW AND STEADY **wins the race to touch the heart of the cantankerous.**

IF YOU AREN'T PRAYING FOR THE MEMBERS OF YOUR FAMILY, who is?

As we scatter kindness, we help to create a safe space where we can openly share the gospel with others. We get to see a life change right before our eyes. Not only the life of another. But our lives as well.

Gift Tags

You have been love bombed!
JOHN 15:17: "This is my command: Love each other."—*Jesus*

You have been love bombed!
JOHN 15:17: "This is my command: Love each other."—*Jesus*

You have been love bombed!
JOHN 15:17: "This is my command: Love each other."—*Jesus*

You have been love bombed!
JOHN 15:17: "This is my command: Love each other."—*Jesus*

2 CORINTHIANS 2:14: "But thanks be to God, who always leads us as captives in Christ's triumphal procession and uses us to spread the aroma of the knowledge of him everywhere."

2 CORINTHIANS 2:14: "But thanks be to God, who always leads us as captives in Christ's triumphal procession and uses us to spread the aroma of the knowledge of him everywhere."

2 CORINTHIANS 2:14: "But thanks be to God, who always leads us as captives in Christ's triumphal procession and uses us to spread the aroma of the knowledge of him everywhere."

2 CORINTHIANS 2:14: "But thanks be to God, who always leads us as captives in Christ's triumphal procession and uses us to spread the aroma of the knowledge of him everywhere."

2 CORINTHIANS 2:14: "But thanks be to God, who always leads us as captives in Christ's triumphal procession and uses us to spread the aroma of the knowledge of him everywhere."

Session Challenges

For your convenience, the six session challenges for this study are printed here. Feel free to photocopy this page on card stock and then cut apart the challenge phrases. You can place the challenge for the current session in your Bible, tape it up on a mirror, or place it on the dashboard of your vehicle or somewhere else that you are sure to see it.

Challenge One: LIVE ALERT.	**Challenge Two:** MAKE THEIR DAY.
Challenge Three: SHARE YOUR STUFF.	**Challenge Four:** LIFT A LONELY, HUG A PORCUPINE, OR SQUEEZE A SKUNK.
Challenge Five: DETONATE A LOVE BOMB.	**Challenge Six:** SCATTER KINDNESS IN SECRET.

Scripture Memory Verses

For your convenience, the memory verses for this study are printed here in the size of a standard business card. Feel free to photocopy this page on card stock and then cut apart the verses. You can then purchase a portable business card holder in which to keep them and carry them with you throughout your day. This way, you can memorize and practice reciting your verses in the car-pool line, waiting room, on lunch hour—any time you have a few spare minutes. Check to see if any members of your group want to arrive early to the sessions to practice reciting the verses from memory for each other.

——— Session 1 ———

In the same way, let your light shine before others, that they may see your good deeds and glorify your Father in heaven.

(MATTHEW 5:16)

——— Session 2 ———

A new command I give you: Love one another. As I have loved you, so you must love one another. By this everyone will know that you are my disciples, if you love one another.

(JOHN 13:34–35)

—— Session 3 ——

Offer hospitality to one another without grumbling. Each of you should use whatever gift you have received to serve others, as faithful stewards of God's grace in its various forms.

(1 PETER 4:9–10)

—— Session 4 ——

The King will reply, "Truly I tell you, whatever you did for one of the least of these brothers and sisters of mine, you did for me."

(MATTHEW 25:40)

—— Session 5 ——

Be kind and compassionate to one another, forgiving each other, just as in Christ God forgave you.

(EPHESIANS 4:32)

—— Session 6 ——

For we are God's handiwork, created in Christ Jesus to do good works, which God prepared in advance for us to do.

(EPHESIANS 2:10)

Listen, Love, Repeat

Other-Centered Living
in a Self-Centered World

Karen Ehman

Because the normal default is to look out for number one, to become a person who thinks about others first will take great effort on our part. It requires us to live alert. To be on the lookout for what Karen Ehman calls "heart drops," stealthily stowed comments in conversations with others that give us a hint into what kindness we might grant them. And also to notice those in our lives who might need a helping hand, a generous dose of encouragement, or a loving gesture done with no expectation of a return favor.

Karen looks at scriptural examples of those who lived alert (among them Abraham, Abigail, the Good Samaritan, and of course Jesus himself, who noticed those who least expected to be noticed). Through these examples, women will be inspired to live alert and to realize that in order to find joy in life, we must learn to stop focusing on ourselves and seek to make someone else's life better instead.

Additionally, this inspiring and practical study provides encouragement and ideas for reaching out to others with both planned and random acts of kindness. Topics include loving your family and friends, encouraging coworkers, reaching out to the lonely, and blessing the "necessary people," those individuals who help you get life done every day but often go unnoticed.

Available in stores and online!

Keep It Shut

What to Say, How to Say It, and When to Say Nothing at All

Karen Ehman

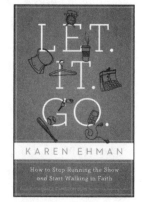

Beyond just a "how not to gossip" book, this book explores what the Bible says about the many ways we are to use our words and the times when we are to remain silent. Karen will cover using our speech to interact with friends, coworkers, family, and strangers as well as in the many places we use our words in private, in public, online, and in prayer. Even the words we say silently to ourselves. She will address unsolicited opinion-slinging, speaking the truth in love, not saying words just to people-please, and dealing with our verbal anger.

Christian women struggle with their mouths. Even though we know that Scripture has much to say about how we are—and are not—to use our words, this is still an immense issue, causing heartache and strain not only in family relationships, but also in friendships, work, and church settings.

A companion video-based study for small groups is also available.

Let. It. Go.

How to Stop Running the Show and Start Walking in Faith

Karen Ehman

Doable ideas, thought patterns, and tools to help you LET GO OF YOUR NEED TO CONTROL
The housework. The meals. The kids. Many women are wired to control. But trying to control everything can be exhausting, and it can also cause friction with your friends and family.

This humorous yet thought-provoking book guides you as you discover the freedom and reward of living a life "out of control," in which you allow God to be seated in the rightful place in your life. Armed with relevant biblical and current examples (both to emulate and to avoid), doable ideas, new thought patterns, and practical tools to implement, *Let. It. Go.* will gently lead you out of the land of over control into a place of quiet trust.

A companion video-based study for small groups is also available.

Available in stores and online!

ZONDERVAN®
.com